Industrial Relations

The Journal of Industrial Relations
Reviewing the World of Work

Mailing address: JIR, School of Business, Faculty of Economics and Business, H10, University of Sydney, NSW 2006, Australia e-mail: jir@econ.usyd.edu.au

Journal of Industrial Relations (ISSN: 0022-1856 print, 1472-9296 online) is published five times a year from 2006 onwards, in February, April, June, September and November by SAGE Publications (London, Thousand Oaks, CA and New Delhi). Annual subscription including postage: institutional rate (combined print and electronic) £280/US$490; special rate Australia: £220/US$385; reduced individual rate (print only) £40/US$70. Electronic only and print only subscriptions are available for institutions at a discounted rate. Visit http://www.sagepublications.com for more details. To activate your subscription (institutions only) visit http://online.sagepub.com. Abstracts, tables of contents and contents alerts are available on this site free of charge for all. Student discounts, single issue rates and advertising details are available from SAGE Publications, 1 Oliver's Yard, 55 City Road, London EC1Y 1SP, UK, tel. +44 (0)20 7324 8500, fax +44 (0)20 7324 8600 and in North America, SAGE Publications, PO Box 5096, Thousand Oaks, CA 91359, USA.

crossref Sage Publications is a member of CrossRef.

US mailing notice: Second class postage applied for at Rahway, NJ.

Abstracting and indexing services: This journal is indexed by APAIS, Business Source Corporate (EBSCO), Business Source Premier (ABSCO) and Emerald Management Services.

Typeset by Regent Typesetting, London and printed on acid-free paper by McPherson's Printing Group, Australia.

The University of Sydney The support of the School of Business at the University of Sydney is gratefully acknowledged.

Industrial Relations

A Current Review

Edited by Richard Hall

SAGE Publications
London • Thousand Oaks • New Delhi

SAGE Publications Ltd
1 Oliver's Yard
55 City Road
London EC I Y I SP

SAGE Publications Inc.
2455 Teller Road
Thousand Oaks, California 91320

SAGE Publications India Pvt Ltd
B-42, Panchsheel Enclave
Post Box 4109
New Delhi 110 017

British Library Cataloguing in Publication data
A catalogue record for this book is available
from the British Library

ISBN-10 1-4129-2950-4   ISBN-13 978-1-4129-2950-9
ISBN-10 1-4129-2951-2   ISBN-13 978-1-4129-2951-6 (pbk)

Library of Congress Control Number: 2006927959

Typeset by Regent Typesetting, London
Printed and bound in Great Britain by
Athenaeum Press, Gateshead
Printed on paper from sustainable resources

Contents

1

Australian Industrial Relations in 2005 – The WorkChoices Revolution

Richard Hall
University of Sydney, Australia

Introduction

This introduction to the 2005 Annual Review edition of the *Journal of Industrial Relations* overviews the major industrial relations development of the year, the introduction of the WorkChoices reform. Many of the contributions which follow analyse the WorkChoices reforms and their particular implications for specific areas of industrial relations practice and policy in greater detail as well as reviewing other key developments throughout the year. Given the significance of the Australian industrial relations reforms announced in 2005, the remainder of this article is devoted to an analysis and assessment of WorkChoices. This edition also provides summaries and assessments of recent industrial relations developments in two other regions – East Asia (in particular, China and Vietnam) and the United Kingdom.

WorkChoices – Rhetoric and Reality

The passing of the WorkChoices reforms by the government-controlled Senate in December 2005 represents the most fundamental revolution in industrial relations since federation. Fundamental industrial relations reform has been a long-held ambition of Prime Minister John Howard. The Government's surprise majority in the Senate secured at the October 2004 federal election provided Howard with the opportunity to realize that ambition. The details of the reforms which emerged in the latter half of the year suggest that he has not squandered the opportunity.

The WorkChoices reforms strongly reflect the personal ideology of Howard. The Prime Minister has long called for fundamental industrial relations and labour market reform and the key elements of his historic mission – greater flexibility in bargaining, decentralization of the industrial relations system, deregulation of the labour market and the restriction of the unfair dismissals jurisdiction – are all addressed in WorkChoices. The personal power of the Prime Minister's position on industrial relations was confirmed by the discipline shown by his Ministers in faithfully repeating his arguments when promoting the reforms throughout the WorkChoices campaign. It also suggests that it might be worth taking a closer look at the rhetoric employed by Howard in fashioning the case for reform.

The rhetoric of the WorkChoices reforms – authored by Howard, disseminated by his government and promoted through a $55million taxpayer-funded advertising campaign – emphasizes themes of 'freedom', 'choice', 'flexibility' and 'fairness'. According to the Minister for Employment and Workplace Relations, Kevin Andrews, WorkChoices accommodates

> ... the greater demand for choice and flexibility in our workplaces. It continues a process of evolution, begun over a decade ago, towards a system that trusts Australian men and women to make their own decisions in the workplace and to do so in a way which best suits them. (Andrews, 2005: 12)

While the WorkChoices rhetoric claims that the reforms directly secure greater freedom, choice and flexibility for employers and employees alike, it turns out that 'fairness' will be achieved indirectly, as a consequence of the new system improving Australia's 'economic strength'. The argument here, developed by Howard in a series of speeches throughout 2005, is that 'fairness at work starts with the promise of a job in the first place'. As Howard has been quick to observe, those are not his words, but 'the words of Tony Blair, a social democrat ...' (Howard, 2005a: 5). According to the rhetoric, by encouraging 'workplace bargaining' and agreement-making WorkChoices will 'strengthen' the Australian economy, which will in turn make it possible for employers to create more jobs and pay higher wages, thus ensuring fairness.

Briggs and Buchanan (2005) have argued that the rhetoric of increased freedom that pervades WorkChoices contrasts starkly with the reality of increased prescriptions and prohibitions. Indeed, the level of detail in the WorkChoices legislation directed toward specifying what can, must and cannot be the subject of bargaining, what can, must and cannot be included in award provisions, as well as the extent of regulation of unions and industrial action is striking. The final version of the *Workplace Relations Amendment (Work Choices) Act 2005* runs to 762 pages and a great deal of other regulation is left to the Regulations to the Act and the discretion of the Minister. Assessing the reforms on the whole, the 'freedom' and 'choice' of the rhetoric turns out to be the freedom of the employer to choose the form of industrial arrangement they prefer, the freedom to decide whether or not they want to make an agreement or leave wages and conditions to the bare minima of the Fair Pay Commission Standards, the freedom to offer individualized Australian Workplace Agreements (AWAs) and the freedom to dismiss workers with less risk of exposure to the unfair dismissals jurisdiction. Employees, for their part, appear to have few new freedoms under WorkChoices, although they now have a greater freedom to trade-off various award conditions or entitlements for other benefits. In formal terms this represents an enhanced freedom to negotiate. In practical terms workers without strong labour market power or without strong collective bargaining more typically confront employers who have designed a set of 'take it or leave it' terms and conditions.

The conception of freedom in WorkChoices is based on the assumption of a relative power balance between the parties in employment relations. In reality, WorkChoices represents a significant repudiation of the logic of labour law itself. In western democracies labour law emerged out of the recognition of the need to protect workers combining in unions to represent their industrial interests and the recognition that labour contracts are qualitatively different from other commercial contracts. The inequality of bargaining power between workers and employers has long been recognized as an axiom of industrial relations and labour law. WorkChoices effectively reduces the scope of labour law in Australia by extending the opportunities for employers to offer jobs with lower pay and poorer conditions, restricting the power of the Australian Industrial Relations Commission (AIRC) to establish and enforce employment standards and reducing the protections and institutional supports traditionally afforded trade unions.

Major Features of WorkChoices

As a number of the contributions to this year's Annual Review edition of the *Journal of Industrial Relations* attest, the changes implied by the WorkChoices reforms are complex, multi-faceted and unlikely to become entirely clear for some time. Nevertheless it is already clear that WorkChoices provides for major changes in six key areas of industrial relations law and practice.

Changing Constitutional Foundation

WorkChoices shifts the constitutional foundation for federal industrial relations legislation from the conciliation and arbitration power to the corporations power. Amongst other things this allows the Commonwealth to directly set minimum terms and conditions of employment without recourse to the making of awards in the settlement of an industrial dispute. The new legislation purports to cover the field of industrial relations and will operate to the exclusion of any state laws with some specified exceptions. However, the federal legislation can only apply to 'constitutional corporations' (trading and financial corporations) and their employees. Unincorporated employers who have operated under a state system will continue to do so, as can employers who are not 'constitutional corporations'. It has been estimated that the corporations power does not cover 15 percent–25 percent of Australian workers (Briggs and Buchanan, 2005). Therefore, contrary to the claims of the Government for a single, national and unified system, state systems will persist albeit in truncated form with much more marginal coverage.

The Rationalization, Freezing and Withering of Awards

No new awards can be created by the AIRC. Existing awards will continue in operation until employers and employees negotiate new agreements. However, these awards will be 'rationalized' such that they are limited to the new 13 allowable award matters and do not include any of the identified non-allowable award matters. Awards are effectively frozen by these reforms. Where current awards have provisions that are more generous than the new five statutory minima (established as the Australian Fair Pay Commission Standards [AFPCS] that apply to all employees) these are preserved but they can not be varied at any time in the future. State awards binding constitutional corporations are absorbed into the new federal system and are treated similarly (for further details see Riley and Sarina in this volume).

Less Regulated Agreement Making and the Removal of the No Disadvantage Test

WorkChoices seeks to simplify the making of agreements (AWAs, employee collective agreements, union collective agreements, employer greenfields agreements and union greenfields agreements) by shortening the period of time required for employers to give notice to employees and introducing a process whereby agreements need only to be lodged rather than certified. Significantly, the no disadvantage test (NDT), whereby agreements could only be certified if they left employees no worse off 'overall' compared to a relevant award, has been removed. In effect, the only protection for employees negotiating (or confronted with) an agreement is provided by the five AFPCS minima.

The Marginalization of the Australian Industrial Relations Commission and the Establishment of the Australian Fair Pay Commission

WorkChoices dramatically recasts the role of the AIRC by all but removing its compulsory arbitral power. Rather than going to the Commission to resolve disputes the parties are required to agree on a dispute resolution procedure of their own. The Commission no longer has any power to make any orders unless it is expressly granted that power in an agreement. The AIRC has therefore also lost its power to hear Safety Net Adjustment cases (and other test cases) and thus lost its power to set effective minimum award wages and other minimum standards. The power to set minimum wages has now been passed to the Australian Fair Pay Commission (AFPC) which has the power to determine its own processes and procedures for setting minima. Commissioners are appointed by the Government for fixed terms. Wage fixing criteria are predicted to focus on narrow macroeconomic considerations (unemployment and inflation) and to no longer make any reference to 'fairness' (Group of 150 Academics, 2005; House of Representatives, 2005). The five basic conditions of employment that constitute the AFPCS are:

4

1. a federal minimum wage of $12.75 per hour (with a 20 percent casual loading);
2. ordinary working hours of 38 hours per week (which can be averaged out over 12 months);
3. four weeks annual leave (of which two weeks can be cashed out);
4. 10 days paid sick leave or carer's leave and two days compassionate leave; and
5. 12 months unpaid parental leave (Stewart, 2005: 13–14).

Increased Regulation of Unions and Industrial Action

The anti-union character of the WorkChoices reforms is underlined by the relatively expansive definition of 'industrial action' applied to union action compared to the comparatively narrow definition applied to employer industrial action. Briggs (2005: 20) has argued that this makes Australia the only OECD country to positively discriminate in favour of lock-outs and against strikes. Protected (ie: lawful) industrial action, which can only be taken during a bargaining period, is now subject to an elaborate set of secret balloting and notice requirements. The Minister can also declare an end to a bargaining period on a wide range of grounds. Union rights of entry to workplaces have also been severely restricted. The exposure of unions, union officials and employees to increased legal sanctions against unprotected action has also been increased (for further details see Barnes this volume).

Restrictions on Employee Protection from Unfair Dismissal

The right of employees to bring an action for unfair dismissal is severely curtailed by the reforms. The right has been eliminated for employees who work for corporations of fewer than 100 employees. Even large employers are protected from the risk of an unfair dismissal claim where they can establish that at least one of the grounds for the dismissal was a 'genuine operational reason'.

The Implications of WorkChoices

While the WorkChoices changes are dramatic it is likely that many of their most profound effects will take some time to become manifest. For example, some of the most pernicious effects will take years to bite at the lower end of the labour market. The combined effect of the freezing and withering of awards, the passing of the minimum wage fixation power to the Fair Pay Commission and the removal of the no disadvantage test for workplace agreements will, in time, lead to lower real and relative wages for Australia's lower paid workers (Watts and Mitchell, this volume). Those 20 percent to 30 percent of workers currently dependent on awards will also suffer a loss of often hard-won industrial conditions as the range of allowable award matters shrinks and award standards stagnate. As those workers are dismissed, made redundant or change jobs they will confront a labour market where many employers are likely prepared to offer only the bare minima of the AFPCS. Realistically, their chances of bargaining a more satisfactory set of conditions and entitlements will depend on their union's ability to overcome the new obstacles to industrial action and collective bargaining and compel their employer to reach a collective agreement rather than unilaterally offer a 'take-it-or-leave-it' AWA – surely an unlikely scenario in the lower paid sectors where unions have traditionally not been strong and where bargaining remains under-developed.

An Expanded Low Wage Sector and Increasing Labour Market Inequality

Lightening the regulation of labour markets, lowering minimum standards to a set of five very basic conditions, establishing an appointed commission to determine a single minimum wage and further weakening trade unions' capacity to negotiate, bargain and fight for higher wages and better conditions will inevitably lead to an expanded low wage sector and lower wages in that sector. This has been the result of similar reforms in New Zealand, Western Australia and Victoria (Briggs, 2005). The resultant increasing labour market inequality will register not just in the form of steadily increasing wage inequality, but also in the form of greater inequalities in conditions and entitlements. Higher paid professional workers with skills in demand will notice little change, although work intensification, long hours and work–family balance dissatisfaction will all continue unabated. Lower paid workers, protected only by the minimal AFPCS, confront the prospect of fewer award standard conditions and benefits, or the prospect of being offered casual or contract work with even fewer protections and entitlements. Workers with certified agreements and strong union representation will be able to continue to try to bargain with their employers. However the removal of award standards, and the increased regulation of union action tilts the industrial playing field further in favour of employers even in unionized sectors. Thus, at the time of writing, Qantas was reportedly in heated negotiations with the unions representing their maintenance workers over the company's plan to effectively roll overtime into standard working hours by averaging the standard 38 hours per week over a six-month period (Rochfort, 2005: 19).

Growth of Individual Contracts and the Contraction of Collective Bargaining

In their submission to the Inquiry into the WorkChoices legislation, the Group of 150 Academics argued that the likely effect of the proposed legislation 'is not so much to promote agreement-making as it is to promote the individualization of the employment relationship' (Group of 150 Australian Academics, 2005: 20). The reforms encourage employers to introduce individual contracts in the form of streamlined AWAs, employer greenfields 'agreements' and common law individual contracts. There are now strong incentives for employers to move workers from awards and certified agreements to these arrangements given that the abolition of the no disadvantage test means that individual agreements, which can obviously be offered on a take-it-or-leave-it basis, need only meet the AFPC standards. In hospitality, retail and health and community services where there are large numbers of award-dependent employees it is highly likely that employers will move quickly to offer standardized, bare minimum AWAs with fewer entitlements such as loadings and penalties. Moreover there appears to be little to stop employers at the expiration of a certified agreement from offering stripped-back AWAs and refusing to negotiate a new collective agreement. Finally, the capacity of unions to resist these trends will be compromised by the new restrictions on organizing at the workplace and industrial action.

Together, lower relative minimum wages and greater use of individual agreements are likely to have particularly adverse consequences for young people, gender pay equity and work and family dynamics (Group of 150 Australian Academics, 2005). The changes will strike hardest at the most vulnerable in the labour market, disproportionately women and youth. Centrally coordinated industrial relations systems are known to produce the fairest outcomes in terms of pay equity for women; the further fragmentation of the system, the further growth in casual work, and the increased use of AWAs and individual contracts will increase gender pay disparities (Watts and Mitchell, this volume). Despite the rhetoric claiming that WorkChoices will facilitate more flexibility and therefore better work and family arrangements, the reforms appear to strengthen the hand of employers, rather than employees, in determining flexible work arrangements. The likely shift over time for many workers from award conditions to arrangements that reflect only the new minimum AFPC standards will exacerbate problems with balancing work and family responsibilities. Workers with care responsibilities also face the prospect of losing award conditions relating to public holidays, rest breaks, and leave, penalty, shift and overtime loadings.

The Corporatization of Australian Labour Law

McCallum (2006) has argued that the changes presage the 'corporatisation of Australian labour law' whereby industrial law becomes a 'subset of corporations law and employees would be regarded as little more than actors in the economic enhancement of corporations'. Under this construction, workers come to be seen not as employees with industrial rights, but as individual contractors whose relationship with their employer is a purely commercial contractual one. Other reforms are entirely consistent with this emerging model: the proposed *Independent Contractors Act* will stimulate the growth of independent contracting rather than employment and facilitate the conversion of at least some workers deemed to be employees to contractor status. Simultaneously, the access of employees to specialist tribunals and commissions has been curtailed under WorkChoices and they are increasingly left to pursue their rights and interests in the regular courts.

Limited Impact on Employment and Unemployment

For all the rhetoric about WorkChoices increasing employment growth, the evidence that can be garnered to support the claims of a positive employment/ unemployment effect associated with the reforms is slight and unconvincing (Watson, 2004). There is some evidence that lower wage rates lead to some increase in job creation, but of course, where they do, the growth is in low paid jobs at the potential expense of at least some high paid jobs. Very large reductions in real wages are required to have any impact on unemployment. There is no evidence that current unfair dismissal laws affect employment rates and there is no evidence that their restriction will increase job creation.

Encouragement of a 'Low Road' Labour Market Development Path

One of the Government's central arguments for WorkChoices is that it will improve productivity. Indeed this is the lynchpin of the WorkChoices logic – the forms of agreement-making that will be encouraged by WorkChoices will lead to more productive workplaces that will enable employers to pay higher wages and employ more people. Setting aside the question of what employers might choose to do with the surpluses generated by productivity improvements, the evidence for the link between level of agreement-making and productivity is limited (Addison and Belfield, 2001; Preston and Crockett, 2004). Productivity growth in Australia did indeed increase in the 1990s following the introduction of enterprise bargaining, as Howard (2005a) in a rare reference to 'evidence' has observed, however as Buchanan (2004) and others have argued this is probably linked to employers' more intensive use of labour under conditions of chronic understaffing. In any event, there is no evidence that productivity is linked to individual contracts. As the submission of the 150 academics argues, Government arguments linking improved productivity to bargaining often conflate individual and collective bargaining under the heading of 'workplace bargaining'. Thus Howard (2005a) refers to BCA research showing that enterprise bargaining firms increased productivity faster than award firms. First, this ignores the impact on productivity of a multitude of other potentially significant variables. Second, enterprise bargaining firms in Australia since the early 1990s have overwhelmingly undertaken collective bargaining rather than individual contracting. WorkChoices, as argued above, works to encourage *individual* contracting rather than *collective* bargaining. Moreover, by facilitating the growth of low paid work, WorkChoices sets Australia more clearly on the 'low road' of labour market development – strong growth in jobs with low skills, low discretion, limited training and development, underdeveloped career paths and limited capacity to add value. Under these conditions employers tend to pursue low cost, rather than high investment, labour usage strategies. Not only is this bad for individual workers in the lower half of the labour market, it is bad for the economy in the long run, and is likely to exacerbate Australia's problems with skill shortages and gaps.

The Politicization of Industrial Relations

While industrial relations is inevitably political, the WorkChoices reforms mark a new level in the executive's control over this area of policy and a new frontier in Howard's politicization of key Australian public institutions. The marginalization of the quasi-judicial and independent Industrial Relations Commission in favour of institutions such as the AFPC and the Office of the Employment Advocate, which are less independent of government, is one of the remarkable features of WorkChoices. Even more alarming is the extent to which the WorkChoices legislation affords significant discretion to the Minister. For example, as highlighted by Riley and Sarina in this volume, s. 356 of the Act gives the Minister unfettered discretion to declare at any time a matter to be 'prohibited content' for the purposes of agreement making and any attempt to include such content in an agreement attracts a fine of $33,000. Added to this is the Ministerial discretion to declare an end to a bargaining period thus rendering any further industrial action unlawful.

As noted at the outset of this analysis, by relying on the corporations power in the Constitution, the Howard Government has opened up the way for more direct regulation of the terms and conditions of employment in Australia than has hitherto been the case. Amongst other things, this also opens up the way for a future government of a different political persuasion to directly legislate on the basis of ILO conventions and to set labour standards that many might see as more appropriate for a modern economy and a civilized society. There would seem no reason why a future Government could not use the AFPC standard as the basic framework for a much more detailed and progressive set of labour standards setting a benchmark for the entire economy, augmented by a more comprehensive set of industry awards.

The WorkChoices reforms represent a new level of politicization of industrial relations in another sense – the legislation almost perfectly implements the key industrial relations reforms proposed by the major employer lobby groups. While the major employer associations have long called for the need for further industrial relations reform, it was only in 2005 as the extent of the Government's willingness to move on IR became apparent that the major employer groups fashioned specific wish lists. As Hearn Mackinnon's chapter in this volume makes clear, the major employer groups were ultimately 'enormously successful' in getting their main proposals implemented. Little wonder perhaps, given that the Department of Employment and Workplace Relations chief counsel conceded that the country's largest law firms, which represent Australia's largest corporations, were seconded to assist the Department in drafting the legislation (Hearn Mackinnon, this volume).

WorkChoices – What's Behind the Rhetoric?

At first glance, then, WorkChoices might appear to be simply a blatant and virulent expression of Realpolitik. Indeed the legislation can be read as a checklist of employer reform proposals and reactions to AIRC and tribunal decisions that have gone against employers. However this may well underestimate the deeper significance of the WorkChoices revolution.

While rhetorical analysis has not been a traditional research method in industrial relations scholarship, a study of the rhetoric employed by Howard in the WorkChoices debate throughout 2005 reveals some distinctive conceptions of the contemporary Australian worker, the role of government and public institutions and the relationship between work and family life.

In a speech on 22 March 2005 Howard argued that substantial industrial relations reform was needed in order to 'consolidate the transition of the Australian economy from an economy governed by a centralized approach to industrialisation [sic] and wage fixation to one that is truly and fully enterprise based'. In a speech on 11 July 2005 Howard linked his notion of the emergent 'enterprise based economy' to his image of the emergent Australian worker, captured in his phrase, 'the rise of the enterprise worker'. In an example of rhetoric that quite remarkably echoes Menzies' famous 'forgotten people' speech of 1942, Howard defines and appeals to this 'new breed' of worker.

> These Australians do not fit neatly into categories based on age, or geography, occupation or industry, income level or formal qualification. They are white collar and blue collar. They work each day in our factories, our small businesses, our great service companies, our farms and our mines. Some choose to be trade unionists, many do not. Most are traditional employees, while a growing number have embraced the independence and flexibility of working for themselves ... [they] include the knowledge workers ... the providers of personalized services reshaping our society with little more than initiative, a mobile phone and a computer... What unites our enterprise workers, and what has helped lift Australia's economic performance, is an attitude of mind. They recognise the logic and fairness of workplaces where initiative, performance and reward are linked together.... They have a long-term focus, knowing that short-term gains without regard to productivity are illusory if the result is inflation and jobs at risk. Most importantly they grasp that high wages and good conditions in today's economy are bound up with the productivity and success of their workplace. (Howard, 2005a: 2)

In this important passage, Howard is using the rhetorical strategy of 'strategic ambiguity' – 'enterprise worker' might be taken to imply a worker who is 'enterprising' in the sense that they have a strong entrepreneurial spirit and sense of self-reliance, or alternatively, a worker who recognizes that their fortunes are tied to the fortunes of the enterprise that employs them. The former construction justifies an industrial relations regime where elaborate protections and industrial rights are regarded as old-fashioned and unnecessary obstacles to entrepreneurial initiative. The latter justifies a privileging of the workplace-cum-corporation as the appropriate site for agreement making and its promotion as the key focus for law and policy. Underlining McCallum's identification of the corporatization of labour law, it follows that Howard sees the advancement of the corporation rather than the protection of the individual worker as the true object of industrial relations policy.

Later in the same speech, Howard draws a distinction between what he terms 'labour market insiders' and 'outsiders'. The former, he suggests, are permanent, full-time, unionized employees who have long been protected by the industrial relations system to the detriment of the 'outsiders' – the unemployed, the battlers, the willing new entrepreneurs who have been shut out of the labour market by archaic industrial relations practices, especially the 'job-destroying unfair dismissal laws'. In similar vein Howard also takes aim at 'the industrial relations club' and praises Gerard Henderson for having been prepared to strip away 'layers of mythology from a system that was failing our country on the scales of prosperity, of fairness and (ultimately) democracy'.

Howard's rhetorical creation of the enterprise worker and the enterprise based economy does not simply end with the new industrial relations system implied by WorkChoices. It also links to his proposed *Independent Contractors Act* which will facilitate the further expansion of the ranks of contractors (Department of Employment and Workplace Relations, 2005), his welfare to work policies which will help feed the labour demand for the increasing number of low paid jobs implied by WorkChoices (Briggs, 2005), and his work and family policies, or lack thereof. In Howard's rhetoric, WorkChoices actually addresses the need for work and family policies. In the first place it promotes a stronger economy and 'economic security is an important ingredient in the enjoyment of a fulfilling family life' (Howard, 2005b: 4). In the second place WorkChoices better allows workers to negotiate at the workplace level the flexible terms and conditions of employment that will permit them to balance work and family. Ironic then that the reality that gives lie to this central rhetorical claim of individual negotiation at the workplace was conceded by one employer representative at the Senate Inquiry who admitted that 'virtually no real bargaining took place in the non-collective stream' (Hearn Mackinnon, this volume).

Ultimately, while Howard relied heavily on rhetoric in promoting the WorkChoices reforms in 2005, his plan amounts to much more than 'mere rhetoric' or political opportunism. An examination of Howard's rhetoric suggests that it is more than just an (unsuccessful) attempt to persuade the electorate. It reveals the place of industrial relations policy in a broader, more encompassing vision of the role of the state, the market and the family. And this – Howard's vision – is the real revolution at the heart of WorkChoices.

Acknowledgement

Thanks to Bradon Ellem, John Buchanan, Chris Briggs, Naomi Fox, Simon Foy and anonymous reviewers.

References

Addison, J. and Belfield, C. (2001) 'Updating the Determinants of Firm Performance; Estimation Using the 1998 UK Workplace Employee Relations Survey', *British Journal of Industrial Relations* 39(3): 341–66.

Andrews, K. (2005) 'Workplace Relations Amendment (Work Choices) Bill 2005 – Consideration of Senate Message' Parliament of Australia, House of Representatives, Hansard. 7 December.

Briggs, C. (2005) *Federal IR Reform: the Shape of Things to Come.* ACIRRT University of Sydney. Commissioned by Unions NSW, November 2005.

Briggs, C. and Buchanan, J. (2005) *WorkChoices: Overview and Likely Implications.* ACIRRT presentation. ACIRRT, University of Sydney, November 2005.

Buchanan, J. (2004) *Paradoxes of Significance: Australia casualisation and labour productivity.* ACIRRT Working Paper no. 93, University of Sydney.

Department of Employment and Workplace Relations (DEWR) (2005) 'Discussion paper: Proposals for Legislative Reform in Independent Contracting and Labour Hire Arrangements', Canberra: Commonwealth of Australia.

Group of 150 Australian Academics (2005) *Research Evidence About the Effects of the WorkChoices Bill.* Submission to the Inquiry into the Workplace Relations Amendment (Work Choices) Bill 2005.

House of Representatives (2005) *Workplace Relations Amendment (Work Choices) Bill 2005 – Explanatory Memorandum.* Parliament of Australia, November.

Howard, J. (2005a) 'Workplace Relations Reform: the Next Logical Step'. Transcript of the Prime Minster. Address to the Sydney Institute, Four Seasons Hotel, Sydney, 11 July. http://www.pm.gov.au/news/speeches

Howard, J. (2005b) 'Address to the Australian Industry Group Annual Dinner'. Transcript of the Prime Minister. The Great Hall, Parliament House, Canberra, 15 August. http://www.pm.gov.au/news/speeches

McCallum, R. (2006) 'Justice at Work: Industrial Citizenship and the Corporatisation of Australian Labour Law', *Journal of Industrial Relations* 48(2).

Preston, A. C. and Crockett, G. V. (2004) 'Worker Participation and Firm Performance', *Journal of Industrial Relations* 46(3): 345–65.

Rochfort, S. (2005) 'Qantas to do battle with workers', *Sydney Morning Herald*, February 7.

Stewart, A. with Priest, E. (2005) 'The Work Choices Legislation: An Overview' in B. Creighton and A. Stewart, *Labour Law.* Sydney: Federation Press.

Watson, I. (2004) 'Minimum Wages and Employment: A Comment', *Australian Economic Review* 37(2): 166–72.

2

The Australian Labour Market in 2005

Martin O'Brien
University of Wollongong, Australia

Richard Denniss
Parliament House, Canberra, ACT

John Burgess
University of Newcastle, Australia

Introduction

There were no dramatic developments in the labour market in 2005; the dramatic developments came in the legislature. There was a continuation of job growth, the official unemployment rate remained at a historical low and labour force participation rates remained stable. In the 12 months to October 2005 the economy created another 230,000 jobs, maintaining the ongoing expansion in jobs and the associated fall in unemployment that that has continued for the past 14 years. What was dramatic in 2005 were developments in government policy with a flurry of legislative activity at the end of 2005 as the government pushed through legislation that changed welfare access and industrial relations. In particular, the WorkChoices industrial relations legislation, while very wide reaching in terms of change, was not supported by any research linking changes in industrial relations legislation to improved economic performance. While $55million was spent on proclaiming the virtues of WorkChoices, it appears that not one dollar was not spent on establishing a case for what is a major legislative change. Equally surprising is that, given the state of the economy, the legislative change seems to have been made on the basis of an implied view that the economy is weak and its performance can be improved by the legislation.

The Economic Context

The economy continued on its growth cycle with real GDP expanding by 2.3 percent in the year to June (see Table 1). Inflation remained just within the

Table 1 *Economic performance 2005*

Indicator, month	Annual change	Comments
Real GDP – June	2.3%	Continued growth, but relatively low given the terms of trade boost.
Inflation – consumer price index – September	3.0%	At the top of the Reserve Bank band, despite increase in oil prices. Main contributions, transport and education.
Terms of trade – October	15%	Significant increase in commodity prices over the past 2 years. Terms of trade are at a 30 year high.
Exchange rate – trade weighted index – October	1.8%	Ongoing appreciation, continuing a longer term trend.
Current account deficit – June	−0.8%	Current account deficit as a ratio of GDP continues to grow, currently 6.7%
House prices – residential – September	1.7%	Slow down as compared to previous years – reduces the pressure on interest rates
Interest rates – November	0.25% increase to 5.5%	Increase in cash rates in March, since stable.
Fiscal balance – June	Forecast to be $11.5b surplus	Continuation of surpluses with growth in jobs, profits, petrol taxes and Telstra dividends.

All data derived from Australian Economic Indicators, Catalogue 1350, ABS, Canberra, December, 2005.

boundaries set by the Reserve Bank of Australia (see Table 1). Housing prices, a concern of recent years, appear to have stabilized. House prices in Sydney, Canberra and Melbourne slightly declined over the past year, however, strong growth was recorded in Brisbane and Perth (Reserve Bank of Australia, 2005a: 28).

The major macroeconomic issue over the past year has been the impact of rising oil prices on economic activity and inflation. Despite an increase in auto petrol prices of 25 percent in the two years to September 2005, the recent decline in oil prices and falling prices for other goods (especially imported electronic goods), have assisted in stabilizing domestic consumer prices (Stevens, 2005).

The current account deficit continues to expand, despite a considerable improvement in the terms of trade (see Table 1). The exchange rate has slightly appreciated, but by not much considering the extent of the terms of trade improvement. The continued strong growth in commodity prices (especially metals and ores), driven by the expansion of the Chinese economy, is the main reason behind the improving terms of trade. The Reserve Bank suggests that the improved terms of trade has added around 1.5 percent to GDP for each of the past two years (Macfarlane, 2005). However, since the improvement is largely mining-based there are few additional jobs created since mining is extremely capital intensive and there is very little up stream processing within Australia. Also, the high foreign ownership of the sector means that many of the gains are remitted as profit and dividend payments abroad. This may be part of the explanation as to why the terms of trade improvement appears to have had a relatively moderate impact on GDP and why the current account deficit continues to grow (see later).

Official interest rates were increased by 0.25 percent in March 2005, largely in response to the high growth in housing prices. Since then interest rates have been stable. At the moment the inflationary pressures of higher oil prices, capacity constraints, the growing current account deficit and the regional housing price boom are being tempered against a slowing down in the economy's growth rate. Fiscal policy also remained stable with the forecast budget surplus increasing to around $11.5billion in 2005/06.

One debate over the state of the economy concerns GDP growth, the improving terms of trade and jobs growth. Jobs growth remained relatively strong (see Table 2) while GDP growth was relatively weak compared to earlier years (see Table 1). Is the official data misleading (Bassenese, 2005)? Why the continuation of jobs growth in the context of lower GDP growth and a stable labour force participation rate? In terms of the GDP and employment relationship the Australian Bureau of Statistics (ABS) (2005) indicates that since GDP leads employment, a slowdown in GDP takes some time to show up in reduced employment growth. The ABS suggests that the lag between GDP and employment turning points of four quarters is longer than the lags experienced in the past (ABS, 2005). Two reasons it suggests for this are the growth in the terms of trade and stability in real unit labour costs. Business has been able to retain and increase employment due to the flow-on effects of the terms of trade improvement and because labour costs have remained stable. This suggests that employment growth will decline and unemployment will increase in 2006 as the jobs market adjusts, with a lag, to the slow down in production.

A related question is why does GDP growth appear to be relatively moderate while the growth in the terms of trade is exceptional? Is there some under-estimation of GDP? (Hall, 2005). The ABS explanation shown earlier implies that the terms of trade effect is not fully captured by GDP growth and this is the case, since GDP is a volume measure and the terms of trade captures the movement in export prices relative to import prices. The Reserve Bank (2005b) points out the difference between GDP and Gross Domestic Income (GDI) – the latter represents the increasing purchasing power of domestic production within the world economy. Improvements in the terms of trade results in GDI being greater than GDP; for the year to December 2004 the Reserve Bank (2005b) estimated that the difference was two percent. The Reserve Bank (2005b) goes on to comment that the recent terms of trade growth has partially been offset by an appreciating exchange rate, a growth in imports and income/

profit remittances abroad and the gains in taxation and royalty payments that accrue to the Federal and state governments. The mining sector, the main beneficiary of the surge in commodity prices, is a relatively small employer of labour and has high levels of foreign ownership. The extent of the leakages from the income gains generated by the terms of trade improvement limits the flow-on effects to employment and jobs in the rest of the economy.

Labour Force Developments 2005

Job expansion continued, the labour force participation rate remained relatively high, the official unemployment rate declined as did the numbers in long term unemployment, job vacancies increased and it was another good year for the labour market. The Reserve Bank (2005a: 31) reported that 'most industries experienced sizeable employment gains over the year to the September quarter'. Behind the aggregate data, previous reviews have pointed out the demographic disparities in labour force participation rates (Burgess, Lee and O'Brien, 2004), the spatially and industrially uneven distribution of jobs growth (Burgess and Mitchell, 2001) and the gap between the unemployment rate and broader measures of labour underutilization (Barret, Burgess and Campbell, 2005).

As in previous years, the majority of additional jobs (125,000) were filled by females. Over the year the male participation rate increased (71.6 percent to 72.1 percent), reversing a longer term trend of decline, while the female participation rate continued its long term expansion (up from 56.3 percent to 57 percent). The part-time employment share continues to expand. While service sector job growth continues to be high in retailing and business and property services, the impact of the booming commodity prices is directly responsible for the lift in mining and construction employment. Utilities, an industry with declining employment over the past decade, have started to increase their employment. The emerging picture is largely a continuation of the trends observed in the labour market over the past decade. The main difference in 2005 is that job growth occurred across all states (even states that have struggled in the past, notably Tasmania and South Australia), and in most industries, including utilities and mining – two sectors with relatively low and declining levels of employment over the past decade.

In the short-term the prospects for the economy and the labour market remain favourable (Reserve Bank of Australia, 2005a). Job vacancies remain relatively high as do hiring intentions (Reserve Bank of Australia, 2005a). Against this, growth in the economy is easing and the current account deficit continues to grow. The IMF (2005) review of the economy reminded the government that the terms of trade could rapidly be reversed. The Westpac review forecast a falling rate of jobs growth in 2006 (Westpac, 2005). The large fiscal surplus provides the government with the opportunity to undertake demand-inducing measures such as tax cuts or increase public expenditure. Of course, WorkChoices is supposed to generate many additional jobs in the short-term,

Table 2 *Key Labour Force Indicators 2005*

Indicator, month	Change	Comment
Employment – November	2.3% growth	Continued expansion in jobs – around 230,000 additional jobs created over the year.
Part time work – November	29% share of work	100,000 additional part time jobs over the year – a growing part time employment share, one of the highest across the OECD.
Employment by state – November	Growth across all states	Highest annual growth in employment in Western Australia (5%). Most additional jobs in Queensland (61,000).
Employment by Industry – August	Strong growth in mining, utilities and construction.	Mining up by 30%; utilities up by 12.6%; property and business services up by 8.3%. Most additional jobs (100,000) in retailing. Declining employment in manufacturing; cultural and recreational services.
Labour force participation rate – November	Up by 0.7% to 64.4%.	Long term increase – rates up for both males and females.
Unemployment rate – November	5.1% – down 0.1%	Lowest official rates over the past 25 years are maintained.
Long term unemployment rate as % of unemployment rate – September	Down from 21.8% to 17.7%	Continued decline in the numbers in long term unemployed and as a share of the official unemployed. Broader measures of labour under utilization declining.
Job vacancies – August	Increase by over 10,000 for the year	Growing number of job vacancies, a rising job vacancy to unemployed ratio.

Source: For November data: The Labour Force, November. Catalogue 6202.0. For August/September/October data, Australian Economic Indicators, Catalogue 1350, December.

largely as a result of the dilution of the application of unfair dismissal protection. We suggest in the following section that many of these claims regarding the impact of WorkChoices on the labour market are fanciful.

WorkChoices and its Likely Impact on the Labour Market

Having gained an unexpected majority in the upper house after the 2004 Federal election the Coalition government set out to achieve a wide range of reforms to the industrial relation system that it had previously been unable to pass. The rationale proposed by the Government for these changes is that they will deliver increases in employment and productivity and in turn deliver lower unemployment and higher economic growth. In addition to the changes represented by the *Workplace Relations Amendment (Work Choices) Bill*, the Government has also implemented a raft of substantial changes to the welfare system in the form of the *Employment and Workplace Relations Legislation Amendment (Welfare to Work and other Measures) Bill* 2005. The focus here will be on the potential employment and productivity effects of WorkChoices. We will also consider the changes to welfare access, since these have to be placed alongside WorkChoices.

There are two notable features of the WorkChoices legislation. First, prior public inquiries and available research evidence do not support it. For a major piece of legislation it is surprising that there is an absence of research material to support the legislation. One could be forgiven for thinking that Australia has very high trade union density, a record of extensive industrial disputation, a high unemployment rate and low productivity growth. The state of the labour market and industrial relations in Australia does not justify extensive legislative change. In this context it is best to see WorkChoices as a largely ideological piece of legislation that regulates trade unions, diminishes the responsibilities of the Australian Industrial Relations Commission (AIRC), erodes the award system and offers expanded choice to employers regarding industrial instruments. Second, it is extremely complex legislation. To some extent the legislation will create many additional jobs in the legal profession as employers, trade unions and employees seek advice on the implications and operation of the legislation.

The WorkChoices legislation is extensive, interventionist and complex. It attempts to centralize industrial relations power with the Commonwealth while maintaining the State's system for state-based public sector workers and those employed in unincorporated enterprises. It creates a new institution, the Australian Fair Pay Commission (AFPC), while at the same time seeking to further marginalize the Australian Industrial Relations Commission (AIRC). It contains extensive transitional arrangements and is designed to have a gradual impact on work and workplaces. The impact of WorkChoices will not be immediate; its effects will filter through the industrial relations system over a number of years. The new industrial relations system involves new layers of regulation and new institutions in addition to the existing regulations and institutions (Bray and Waring, 2005). The legislation does not represent a simplification of the industrial relations system (Stewart, 2005) and doubts over its constitutionality add uncertainty to the new system (Shaw and Coilek, 2005).

The government justifies WorkChoices largely in terms of additional jobs and increased productivity emanating from the legislative changes (Andrews, 2005a). There is very little evidence supporting a linkage between changes in industrial relations arrangements and economic performance. The Calmfors and Driffil (1988) model suggested improved macroeconomic performance was linked to either complete centralization or complete decentralization of wage determination arrangements. Subsequent evaluation of the link between bargaining systems and macroeconomic performance by the OECD (1997) indicated that the evidence was very weak and that the linkage between systems of bargaining and macroeconomic performance had to consider intermediate linkages including the degree of unionization and the co-ordination of wage setting. As Traxler (1998) noted, bargaining systems require supporting institutions. What was revealed by the OECD (1997) study was that a more decentralized system was generally conducive to greater wage inequality since it awarded wage increases to those with bargaining power (Preston and Burgess, 2003). Blau and Kahn (1999) suggest that institutions have a greater impact on the distribution of wages than on levels of employment. Centralized wage setting institutions compress wage relativities, improve the relative pay of the low paid and reduce the gender earnings gap. Evidence on employment effects is mixed and usually discussed in terms of levels of severance pay, unemployment benefits and the rigidity of the wage structure (Blau and Kahn, 1999). In all of this the bargaining system is only one of many labour institutions and policies that are operating in an economy.

An executive minute from the Treasury (2005, attachment B) on the economic case for the WorkChoices legislation listed the case for reform as follows:

- significant increases in the minimum wage have a negative effect on unemployment – the employment elasticity of a wage increase is around 0.4;
- reducing the potential for unfair dismissal claims will encourage more employment;
- employers will respond to reduction in workplace complexity by increasing employment;
- minimum wage increases are likely to be lower under the AFPC as compared to the AIRC and this will increase employment growth; and
- short-run stagnation of productivity growth as low paid (and relatively unskilled) employment expands, but with longer term positive impact on productivity as firms achieve better matching of workers with positions and adopt new technologies and management practices.

The minute from the Treasury (2005) makes it clear that it has never undertaken any modeling of the effects of WorkChoices on the economy nor has it written any report on such modeling. In effect it is setting out, in the absence of any evidence, what arguments could be put in support of WorkChoices. This case is a curious mix of wishful thinking and revealing insights about WorkChoices. As for wishful thinking it is not clear how the deployment of labour, new technology or new management practices are constrained by the present industrial relations system and how these factors are liberated by the new system. Also, we again see the assumption that the watering down of unfair dismissal will open the floodgates to new jobs growth. We also see the claim that the legislation reduces complexity but it is far from clear how complexity is reduced. What is revealing are the claims that more jobs will be created since wage growth will now be lower, principally because the AFPC will deliver lower wage increases than the AIRC.

Apart from the unpublished Treasury minute, it is difficult to find any analysis from the Government to support its economic claims about WorkChoices (Gittins, 2005). Our interpretation of WorkChoices, in terms of wage and labour cost outcomes, is that it seeks to:

- reduce conditions and standards of employment for some workers, generally the low paid and the award dependent, through the application of the AFPCS (Waring, de Ruyter and Burgess, 2005); and
- reduce minimum wages over time in real terms and relative to median wages through the creation of the AFPC with its primary objective being the linking of minimum wage adjustments to its employment effects (Waring, de Ruyter and Burgess, 2006).

The consideration of present awards and an assessment of how they may look under the WorkChoices arrangements supports the first claim. In many cases it will mean either reduced pay and/or reduced conditions (Waring, Burgess and de Ruyter, 2005). Under the previous 'no disadvantage test', employees could expect that proposed agreements would be compared with the totality of award pay and conditions. Under the AFPCS, agreements will be measured only against a minimum ordinary pay rate and a few leave provisions. New agreements will be registered even when they push total earnings for employees below award levels. Wages and conditions for some workers are likely to diminish given a bargaining environment where there is reduced access to unfair dismissal remedies, where there is a right for employers to unilaterally replace agreements with the AFPCS after their expiry, and where Australian Workplace Agreements (AWAs) can prevail over collective agreements and awards.

With respect to the second claim, a review of recent safety net wage decisions by the AIRC reveals decisions that have been well above those supported by the Federal government and the main employer groups (O'Neill, 2005). There is the suggestion that the decisions have been excessive and have not considered their potential to erode employment. Submissions to the Senate hearing into WorkChoices by employer associations are more explicit about the failings of the AIRC safety net adjustments. The Australian Chamber of Commerce and Industry (ACCI, 2005) argued that minimum wage levels in Australia are the highest in the world in purchasing power and relative terms, that the coverage of the safety net extends beyond those on minimum wages, that recent increases are extravagant relative to changes in the cost of living, and that the AIRC is not considering criteria that is relevant to job generation and competitiveness. In its submission to the Senate inquiry the ACCI stated that national wage cases have 'become highly confused in regard to the importance of wage fixing taking into account the needs of the unemployed ... they have also yielded an unsatisfactory, unduly legalistic, and economically unsound treatment of economic materials' (ACCI, 2005: 35). This implies an expectation that the AFPC will be delivering lower wage increases than the AIRC, and will be delivering these increases to fewer workers (see the above

Treasury minute). As a consequence, both the real and relative wage of the low paid will decline over time.

On the issue of job generation, how is WorkChoices going to generate additional jobs? We suggest the paths through which this will be achieved include: improved procedural flexibility in job hiring through the removal of unfair dismissal provisions for organizations with fewer than 100 employees; reduced labour costs over time through the combined operation of the AFPCS and AFPC; and changes in the wage structure, with the relative pay of the low paid declining over time.

With respect to unfair dismissal exemptions it has long been claimed that such laws inhibit hiring. For example, in 2002 it was estimated that 77,842 jobs would be created if small business was exempted from the unfair dismissal laws (Harding, 2002). This estimate has, however, been subject to widespread criticism. For example, in evidence to the Senate Employment, Workplace Relations and Education Committee (2005) inquiry into unfair dismissal and small business employment it was suggested that this number was based on a 'quick and dirty opinion survey' (Dr Paul Oslington cited in Senate Employment, Workplace Relations and Education Committee 2005: 2). A review of available evidence by Robbins and Voll (2005) reported that there was no consistent evidence linking unfair dismissal to a reluctance to hire in the small business sector. There is already a class of employee who is excluded from unfair dismissal provisions – casual workers. They have a relatively high density in the small business sector (Campbell and Burgess, 2001). There is no evidence that small business has in the past been inhibited from hiring labour due to the presence of unfair dismissal legislation. Indeed, in their review of unfair dismissal protection, Freyens and Oslington (2005, 64) stated that:

> If, as advocated by the government, the main reason for the removal of unfair dismissal protection is to create a large number of jobs, one would normally expect the proposal to be backed by sound evidence about the negative impact of the existing provisions. This is clearly not the case.

Can lower real and relative wages for the low paid deliver more jobs? The complexity of the legislation and the long transition period will mean that there will be no immediate employment impact. This is a program designed to reduce real and relative wages at the lower end of the earnings distribution and remove many non-wage benefits through diluting awards and forcing more workers onto AWAs over time. This will not happen evenly across all workplaces and all organizations, since local labour market conditions will place a limit on change, as will employers' desire to retain an existing workforce and employee commitment. Whether additional jobs will be created in low wage sectors is debatable since it seems that the AFPCS has the potential to allow for better matching of labour use with labour demand and to extend the working hours of the existing workforce without limitations being placed on working hours or by penalty rates. While WorkChoices has the potential to reduce real labour costs in time, it seems its main appeal for employers is to the opportunity it affords them to get more out of existing workers. In this context, work intensification and longer hours will not be job-generating, but potentially job-reducing. With fewer controls over labour deployment as a result of the erosion of the award system and the further dilution of basic conditions, it seems possible that more work can be extracted from existing workers and with better intertemporal deployment of labour. In this context there may be fewer jobs, especially part-time and casual. The experience of greater decentralization of bargaining in Australia is one of increased numeric flexibility of the workforce and longer hours, many of them unpaid over-time (Campbell, 2002). WorkChoices continues this process, for example, through setting full-time weekly hours as an average over the year. There may be some substitution effects, at the margin, between part-time and full-time workers, and between lower-paid workers (youth and disabled workers) and adult workers. With substitution between different classes of employees the scope for job generation is reduced. The case for the changes being job-generating has not been made. If you accept that more low paid jobs will be created in the economy, then it becomes difficult to demonstrate productivity improvements (see below).

What about higher rates of labour productivity being generated by Work Choices?

The National Farmers Federation has argued that the reforms will increase productivity and flexibility (NFF, 26 May 2005). On the productivity issue we can say that there is no evidence linking industrial relations legislative changes to sustained productivity gains (Wooden, 2001: 255) and that the WorkChoices legislation appears to part of the ongoing process of extracting more effort and hours out of the existing workforce. That is, it can generate improvements in the utilization of the existing workforce but does not address the issue of raising the productive capacity of the economy through time. There has been an ongoing debate about the extent and sources of productivity gains in Australia over the 1990s (Hancock, 2005; Parnham, 2003, 2005; Quiggin, 2001). In these debates industrial relations legislative changes do not figure as one of the main contributors. Burgess and Waring (2005) considered the issue of productivity and WorkChoices and they suggest that by permitting employers to reduce wages and conditions, especially for the relatively low paid, WorkChoices will be encouraging employers to pursue a cost minimization strategy in which employers are unlikely to invest in firm-specific training or upgrade their capital stock. This process will be reinforced by the expected reduction in minimum wage increases through the AFPC. This provides incentives for low wage and low skill employment and an increase in the labour intensity of production, and may potentially reduce productivity growth in the long term (Lowe, 1996). In his review of the link between bargaining instruments and productivity, Peetz (2005) could not find any link between decentralized instruments such as AWAs and improved productivity performance.

It also seems that other problems facing the economy such as a skills shortage and an ageing workforce are totally ignored, even exacerbated by WorkChoices. There is nothing in WorkChoices to strengthen employer-provided training, indeed the cost minimization strategies by WorkChoices appear to be inimical to longer-term workplace investment. As for an ageing workforce and improving retention and making work more attractive, it again appears that WorkChoices is largely silent, even detrimental to improving work–life balance (Group of 150 Australian Academics, 2005).

WorkChoices and Welfare to Work Changes

WorkChoices cannot be divorced from the changes to welfare access. The main objective of the *Employment and Workplace Relations Legislation Amendment (Welfare to Work and other Measures) Bill* 2005 was to place stricter criteria on recipients of the disability support pension (DSP) and the parenting payment (PP) with a view to encouraging greater labour force participation. Under the new arrangements the definition of 'work' has been changed such that in order to receive DSP an individual's disability would now need to be such that it prevented them from working 15 hours per week, as opposed to the earlier test of 30 hours per week. This new test will only be applied to new applicants for DSP, hence the long transition associated with the process of implementation.

The DSP is more generous than the New Start Allowance and it is estimated that the reduction in the number of people receiving the DSP will deliver savings of $2.3 billion over the period 2006–07 to 2008–09 (Department of Parliamentary Services 2005: 3). These savings will, however, be more than offset by increased expenditure on employment placement assistance. In supporting the need for these changes the Minister for Employment and Workplace Relations, Kevin Andrews stated:

> This bill will respond to our twin challenges: the imperatives to increase participation for these groups and reduce their level and incidence of welfare dependence. (Andrews, 2005b)

As with the industrial relations legislation described earlier there is a paucity of empirical or theoretical evidence to support the claim that substantial economic benefits will flow from the tightening of access to disability and parenting payments.

In articulating the rationale for the changes Minister Andrews focused on the importance of ensuring that disabled people have access to the benefits associated with paid employment. It is important to note, however, that individuals in receipt of DSP were not constrained from seeking paid employment. While the Government has focused on the importance of increasing the incentive for those in receipt of DSP, there has been no evidence presented to support the assumption that employers are eager to employ individuals with disabilities. In fact, recently released data shows that the Commonwealth Government is itself employing substantially fewer individuals with disabilities. For example, across the entire Commonwealth public service the proportion of employees with disabilities has declined from 5.6 percent in 1996 to 3.8 percent in 2004. In the Department of Prime Minister and Cabinet, the department responsible for the co-ordination and implementation of government policy, the proportion of employees with disabilities has declined from 4.6 percent to 2.2 percent over the same period (Abetz, 2005).

The welfare changes support WorkChoices since it prevents employees leaving jobs if they are unhappy with wages and conditions, and moving on to unemployment benefits since voluntary separation will reduce access to unemployment benefits. At the same time the government has admitted that job seekers must accept the first available job, in order to stay on benefits, even if the jobs has sub-award wages and conditions (Seccombe, 2005). Together with the elimination of unfair dismissal legislation the prerogative of employers is significantly strengthened. Horin (2005) suggests that the industrial relations and welfare legislation will create a 'pool of low paid wage slaves'.

Conclusion

The Australian labour market recorded another year of strong job growth and the official unemployment rate remained at a historically low level. Jobs growth was spread across most states and industries. Against this background it is surprising that the Federal government has introduced radical legislation that appears to be premised on a state of affairs in the economy and the workplace that does not exist. The immediate economic impact of WorkChoices is difficult to analyse due to the long period of transition and the uncertainties as to how employers will respond to the opportunities presented to them by WorkChoices. On balance, we suggest that the relative pay and conditions for the low paid will decline, that wage inequality in the economy will expand, there will be growing numbers of working poor, that the employment effects are likely to be minimal and the impact on short term productivity will be positive, but negative in the longer term.

References

Abetz, E. (2005) Answer to a Question on Notice from Senator Kerry Nettle, July 25 2005, Question 1038.

Andrews, K. (2005a) 'A New Workplace Relations System: A Plan for a Modern Workplace', Media Release, 26 May.

Andrews, K. (2005b) Second Reading Speech Employment And Workplace Relations Legislation Amendment (Welfare To Work And Other Measures) Bill 2005, November 9.

Australian Chamber of Commerce and Industry (ACCI) (2005) Submission to the Senate Inquiry into Work Choice Legislation. Canberra.

Australian Bureau of Statistics (ABS) (2005) 'The Terms of Trade and the National Accounts'. *Australia Now*, November 12.

Barrett, S., Burgess, J. and Campbell, I. (2005) 'The Australian Labour Market in 2004', *Journal of Industrial Relations* 47(2): 133–50.

Bassanese, D. (2005) 'The Statistics Don't Lie', *Australian Financial Review*, October 17: 26.

Blau, F. and Kahn, L. (1999) 'Institutions and Laws in the Labor Market', in O. Ashenfelter and D. Card (eds) *Handbook of Labour Economics*, pp. 1399–1558. Amsterdam: North Holland.

Bray, M. and Waring, P. (2005) '"Complexity" and "Congruence" in Australian Labour Regulation', *Journal of Industrial Relations* 47(1): 1–15.

Burgess, J. and Mitchell, W. (2001) 'The Australian Labour Market in 2000', *Journal of Industrial Relations* 43(2): 124–47.

Burgess, J. and Waring, P. (2005) 'The Productivity Question', in C. Shiel (ed.) *The State of the States*, pp. 53–65. Sydney: Evatt Foundation.

Burgess, J., Lee, J. and O'Brien, M. (2004) 'The Australian Labour Market 2003', *Journal of Industrial Relations* 46(2): 160–83.

Calmfors, L. and Driffil, I. (1988) 'Bargaining Structures, Corporatism and Macroeconomic Performance', *Economic Policy*, April: 14–61.

Campbell, I. (2002) 'Extended Working Hours in Australia', *Labour and Industry* 13(1): 91–110.

Campbell. I. and Burgess, J. (2001) 'Casual Employment in Australia and Temporary Employment in Europe: Developing a Cross–National Comparison', *Work, Employment and Society* 15(1): 171–84.

Department of Parliamentary Services (2005) Bills Digest, Employment and Workplace Relations Legislation Amendment (Welfare to Work and Other Measures) Bill 2005, Bills Digest no. 70, December 6 2005.

Freyens, B. and Oslington, P. (2005) 'The Likely Employment Impact of Removing Unfair Dismissal Protection', *Journal of Australian Political Economy* 56: 56–65.

Gittins, R. (2005) 'Porkies Used to Support Industrial Relations Reforms', *Sydney Morning Herald*, February 14: 38.

Group of 150 Australian Academics (2005) *Research Evidence About the Effects of the WorkChoices Bill*. Submission to the Inquiry into the Workplace Relations Amendment (Work Choices) Bill 2005.

Hall, A. (2005) 'Statistical Veil Conceals $16b', *Australian Financial Review*, November 14: 23.

Hancock, K. (2005) 'Productivity Growth 1964/5 to 2003/4', *Australian Bulletin of Labour* 31(1): 28–32.

Harding, D. (2002) *The Effect of Unfair Dismissal Laws on Small and Medium Sized Businesses*. Melbourne: Melbourne Institute of Applied Economic and Social Research.

Horin, A. (2005) 'The One-strike Rule Set to Catch Both Sides Out', *Sydney Morning Herald*, December 10: 33.

International Monetary Fund (IMF) (2005) 'Staff Report for Article IV: Australia', August 24.

Lowe, P. (1996) 'Labour Productivity and Relative Wages, 1978–1994', in P. Anderson, J. Dwyer and D. Gruen (eds) *Productivity and Growth*, pp. 93–134. Sydney: Reserve Bank of Australia.

Macfarlane, I. (2005) 'Global Influences on the Australian Economy. Address to Australian Institute of Company Directors', June 14, Sydney.

National Farmers Federation (NFF) (2005) 'Workplace Relations Reform Agenda will Deliver Flexibility and Productivity', Media release, May 26.

OECD (1997) *Employment Outlook*. Paris: OECD.

O'Neill, S. (2005) 'National Wage and Safety Net Claims and Outcomes 1991–2005', Parliamentary Library Briefing Paper, Canberra.

Parnham, D. (2003) 'Australia's 1990s Productivity Surge and its Determinants', Revised draft of a paper given to the National Bureau of Economic Research, 13th Annual East Asian Seminar on Economics, Melbourne 20–22 June 2002.

Parnham, D. (2005) 'Australia's 1990s Productivity Surge: A Response to Keith Hancock's Challenge', *Australian Bulletin of Labour* 31(3): 295–303.

Peetz, D. (2005) 'Hollow Shells: the Link Between Individual Contracting and Productivity Growth', *Journal of Australian Political Economy* 56: 32–55.

Preston, A. and Burgess, J. (2003) 'Enterprise Bargaining and Economic Pertformance', in
    J. Burgess and D. Macdonald (eds) *Developments in Enterprise Bargaining in Australia*, pp.
    176–194. Melbourne: Tertiary Press.

Quiggin, J. (2001) 'The Australian Productivity Miracle: A Sceptical View', *Agenda* 8(4):
    333–48.

Reserve Bank of Australia (2005a) 'Statement on Monetary Conditions', November.

Reserve Bank of Australia (2005b) 'Commodity Prices and the Terms of Trade'. Reserve
    Bank Bulletin. April: 1–7.

Robbins, W. and Voll, G. (2005) 'The Case for Unfair Dismissal Reform: a Review of the
    Evidence', *Australian Bulletin of Labour* 31(3): 237–54.

Seccombe, M. (2005) 'Jobless Told They Must Accept Work Conditions', *Sydney Morning
    Herald*, October 24: 5.

Senate Employment, Workplace Relations and Education Committee (2005) Inquiry into
    Unfair dismissal and small business employment, 21 June 2005, http://www.aph.gov.au/
    Senate/committee/eet_ctte/unfair_dismissal/report/index.htm

Shaw, J. and Coilek, M. (2005) 'The Constitutional Question', in C. Shiel (ed.) *The State of
    the States*, pp. 45–52. Sydney: Evatt Foundation.

Stevens, G. (2005) 'Economic Conditions and Prospects October 2005'. Address to
    Tasmanian Chamber of Commerce and Industry. Hobart, October 11.

Stewart, A. (2005) 'A Simple Plan for Reform? The Problem of Complexity in Workplace
    Regulation', *Australian Bulletin of Labour* 31(3): 210–36.

Traxler, F. (1998) 'Collective Bargaining in the OECD: Developments, Preconditions and
    Effects', *British Journal of Industrial Relations* 4(2): 207–26.

Treasury (2005) 'Executive Minute', Workplace Relations Policy Announcement.

Waring, P., de Ruyter, A. and Burgess, J. (2005) 'Advancing Australia Fair: the Australian
    Fair Pay and Condition Standard', *Journal of Australian Political Economy* 56: 105–25

Waring, P., de Ruyter, A. and Burgess, J. (2006) 'Work Choices and the Systematic Erosion
    of Employment Standards in Australia', AIRAANZ Conference, Adelaide, February 3–4.

Westpac (2005) 'Australian Labour Market Firm, but Trends Easing', www.westpac.com.au
    accessed August 11 2005.

Wooden, M. (2001) 'Industrial Relations Reform in Australia: Causes, Consequences and
    Prospects', *Australian Economic Review* 34(3): 243–62.

3

Wages and Wage Determination in 2005

Martin J. Watts
University of Newcastle, Australia

William Mitchell
University of Newcastle, Australia

Introduction

This article reviews Australian wage outcomes in 2005 and institutional and legislative developments which will influence future wage determination and employment conditions. The latter has been dominated by the passing of the WorkChoices legislation in December which has destroyed the test-case process for the determination of wages and conditions, along with the system of arbitrated industry based awards (Riley and Sarina, this volume). The state of the macro-economy in 2005 is reviewed prior to analysing wage outcomes. We outline the 2005 legislative changes and speculate on their consequences for future wage outcomes.

Macroeconomic background

The Australian economy grew by 2.6 percent per annum to June 2005 with employment growing by 3.4 percent over the same period (Reserve Bank of Australia, 2005: 25, 32). Unemployment stood at 5.1 percent in November 2005 (ABS, 2005a) but with rising underemployment and hidden unemployment the official measure seriously underestimates total labour underutilization.

The average annualized wage increase per employee associated with newly certified Federal agreements (AAWI) was 4 percent to September 2005. However, the Labour Price (formerly Wage Cost) Index increased 4.2 percent over the same period, compared to 3.5 percent in the year to September 2004, which suggests that skill shortages could be impacting on wage settlements (see below). The annual inflation rate of 3.0 percent to September 2005 was at the top of the Reserve Bank's acceptable range (ABS, 2005d:1). The single interest rate increase of 25 basis points in March 2005 appeared to have slowed the housing market (RBA, 2005: 25), with prices having stabilized in early 2004 (RBA, 2005).

The debt-servicing costs associated with household borrowing rose to 9.8 percent of disposable income in the June quarter, from about 6 percent in 1996 (RBA, 2005: 26). As noted in previous reviews, financial over-commitment by some home buyers, which increased the mal-distribution of household indebtedness, has left many families vulnerable to moderate interest rate increases and/or job loss (Watts and Mitchell, 2004: 161). The Federal government's pursuit of large budget surpluses has forced dissaving on the private sector. There is evidence that the private sector is trying to repair their balance sheets by positive saving which will then bring the fiscal drag inherent in the surpluses into play and unemployment will rise sharply.

Wage Determination in 2005

This section considers the 2005 wage outcomes, including the final decision by the Australian Industrial Relations Commission (AIRC) on the safety net adjustment.

Coverage of Agreements

The Australian Bureau of Statistics (ABS) publication, *Survey of Employee Earnings and Hours* (Cat. 6306.0), reports that in May 2004, 20 percent of all employees were on awards only, representing 24.7 percent of private sector employees and approximately 2.3 percent of public sector employees, as compared to 20.5 percent in 2002 and 23.2 percent in 2000, 38.3 percent of all employees were covered by collective agreements (24.2 percent and 91.8 percent respectively), compared to 36.7 percent in 2000 (ABS, 2004: 25).

The number of Australian Workplace Agreements (AWAs) approved per month stabilized at about 17,000 during 2005 including those approved by the AIRC (see Figure 1) (OEA, 2005b). By 30 September 2005, 487,900 workers (5.7 percent of salary and wage earners) had extant agreements, which represented an annual increase of 34 percent, albeit from a low base (OEA, 2005a, 2005b). AWAs were most likely to cover employees in retail, manufacturing, accommodation, cafes and restaurants and property and business services. Only 12 percent of current AWAs covered firms with less than 20 employees. The private sector accounted for 87.4 percent of the AWAs approved to September 2005 (OEA, 2005a: 1).

Some 1,570,100 workers were covered by registered agreements and 175,300 by non-union certified agreements on 30 June (OEA, 2005a: 3). The highest percentage of employees covered by a union certified agreement were in retail trade, government administration and defence and education, whereas the highest percentage of employees covered by Non-union Agreements were in manufacturing, retail and finance and insurance. A total of 1,750,100 employees were covered by Certified Agreements at the end of September, following

Figure 1   *Monthly Australian Workplace Agreement approvals and quarterly moving average, December 2002–November 2005*

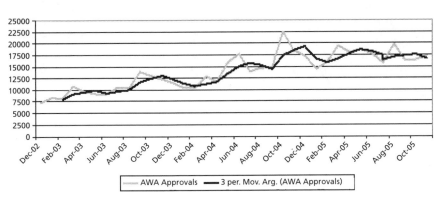

Source: OEA (2005a).

the certification of an additional 1881 agreements covering 169,900 employees (DEWR, 2005a).

Money Wage Growth

Since enterprise bargaining commenced, aggregate wage data have been difficult to interpret. Many employees have unregistered agreements and wage increases may be granted in exchange for trade-offs with respect to other conditions. Also there are major compositional changes occurring in the workforce (Burgess, 1995). Comprehensive data on AWA outcomes are not available, but see below for details.

The Department of Employment and Workplace Relations (DEWR) records the average annualized wage increase (AAWI) per employee based on Federal agreements newly certified within each quarter (see Figure 2). There is no evidence of a sustained increase in wage settlements with the current weighted increases over each of the four quarters to September 2005 for newly certified agreements being approximately 4 percent (DEWR, 2005a: 2), which coincided with the AAWIs associated with all extant agreements (DEWR, 2005a: 3). Likewise ACIRRT found AAWIs of about 4 percent for state and federal certified agreements registered in the four quarters to September 2005 (ACIRRT, 2005).

Full-time adult Average Weekly Earnings grew 6.2 percent in the year to August 2005 which was the same as for the corresponding period in 2004 (ABS, 2005b: 6). The data conflate changes in hourly wages, full-time hours and compositional changes. The growth in Average Weekly Ordinary Time Earnings (which excludes the impact of changes in the overtime component of hours, but reflects compositional changes) was 6.3 percent over the same period (5.7 percent in the year to August 2004) (ABS, 2005b:6).

Figure 2 *Average annualized wage increase (AAWI) per employee of federal agreements newly certified within the quarter by industry group, March 1998–September 2005*

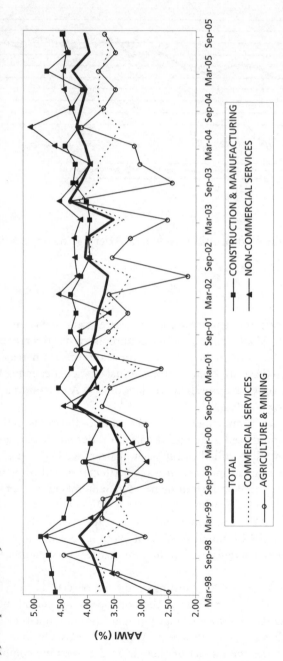

Source: DEWR (2005a) and author's calculations.

Notes: Manufacturing and *Construction* are equivalent to the ANZSIC industries. *Commercial services* consists of wholesale; retail; accommodation, cafes, restaurants; transport; communications; electricity, gas and water; finance and insurance; property and business; cultural and recreation; and personal and other. *Non-commercial services* denote education and health; government administration and defence; and community services. The estimates have been rounded since June 1999. Historical estimates have been updated so that figures may exhibit slight differences as compared to Figure 2 in Watts and Mitchell (2005). The AAWIs are calculated as a weighted sum of the AAWIs per employee per ANZSIC industry with the weights given by the corresponding employment shares.

In the 12 months to September 2005, wage growth, as measured by the fixed weight Labour Price, formerly Wage Cost, Index, grew 4.2 percent seasonally adjusted (see Table 1), compared to 3.5 percent over the previous year (ABS, 2005c: 6).[1] The sharpest increases have occurred in mining, wholesale, transport and storage, health and community services and cultural and recreational services. The DEWR Skilled Vacancy Indexes (SVI) for Health Professionals and Medical and Science Associate Professionals have increased significantly (DEWR, 2005c), but the other occupations cannot be easily mapped into corresponding industries. With the exception of Wholesale and Transport and Storage, these industries experienced sharp increases in employment over the year. ACIRRT (2005: 6) note that employers can address wage pressures from skill shortages through promotion structures, performance bonuses or other methods which are not recorded in enterprise agreements. Also, specific initiatives to address the shortages such as training and improved retention can be adopted.

Skill Shortages and Wage Pressures

Although the labour market has tightened in recent years, there is still only anecdotal evidence that a 'skills shortage' is constraining growth and that wage pressures are intensifying. The Australian Chamber of Commerce and Industry (ACCI) cite skills shortages as one of the most significant barriers to investment in Australia (EWRERC, 2003: 12).

In Figure 3 (panel a) the SVI is shown from the earliest available period (July 1983) to November 2005, and in panel (b) the same index from January 1990 to November 2005. The lower horizontal line in panel (b) is the average value over the period 1990–2005 (97.9) while the upper horizontal line is the average

Figure 3   *DEWR Skilled Vacancy Index, Australia, various periods*

a)

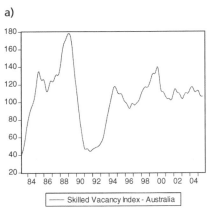

b)

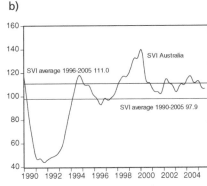

Source: DEWR (2005b).
Note: (a) 1983–2005 and (b) 1990–2005

Table 1 *Annual percentage increases in ordinary time hourly rates of pay index, excluding bonuses, by industry, September 2001–September 2005*

	Sept-01	Sept-02	Sept-03	Sept-04	Sept-05
Mining	2.9	4.2	2.8	3.3	5.0
Manufacturing	3.8	3.5	3.4	3.9	3.7
Electricity, gas and water supply	4.4	4.1	4.1	4.8	4.5
Construction	3.6	3.0	3.9	4.5	4.7
Wholesale trade	3.1	3.4	2.9	2.8	4.0
Retail trade	2.3	3.2	2.7	3.3	3.8
Accommodation, cafes and restaurants	3.1	2.9	3.2	2.4	3.2
Transport and storage	3.2	2.3	4.0	2.8	3.9
Communication services	4.0	2.9	3.2	3.2	3.2
Finance and insurance	3.7	3.6	3.4	3.8	4.3
Property and business services	4.4	3.3	3.3	3.0	3.4
Government administration and defence	3.5	3.0	4.6	4.0	5.0
Education	4.3	3.8	3.8	4.8	4.5
Health and community services	3.4	3.0	4.9	3.1	5.0
Cultural and recreational services	3.1	3.5	4.0	2.9	5.0
Personal and other services	3.4	3.5	3.6	3.5	4.0
All industries	3.7	3.1	3.6	3.5	4.2

Source: Australian Bureau of Statistics (ABS, 2005c: Table 6; ABS, 2003).

value over the period 1996–2005 (111.0). The charts provide no aggregate level indication that there has been a sharp rise in the demand for skills in the last several years.

Mitchell and Quirk (2005) find that: (a) The SVI for tradespersons rose sharply over 2003 and 2004 but declined over the last 18 months. The Professions (since 2001) and Associate Professions (since 1998) have been in trend decline; (b) For Professions and Associate Professions, only the health sector has experienced rapid growth in the SVI in 2005. A relevant issue is the number of immigrants who have foreign nursing or medical qualifications and are not practising in this country as a result of local certification constraints (Hawthorne, 2001); and (c) Skilled vacancies in both NSW and Victoria reveal worsening trends and the recent growth areas of Queensland and Western Australia are now negative (QLD) and flat (WA).

Australian Workplace Agreements

It is instructive to examine the manner in which AWAs are finalized, as well as their content, since the thrust of the industrial relations reforms is to facilitate their introduction. The government claims that individual contracts will provide employers and employees with increased choice and flexibility, with the latter associated with higher productivity. Contrary to the Federal Coalition (2004: 5), there is little evidence of employees having any input into the structure and conditions of their AWAs, with 35 percent of employers not consulting with workers (Gollan, 2000) and some employees having no option to negotiate (Van Barneveld and Waring, 2002). An 'overwhelming proportion' of AWAs were based on short-term cost reduction rather than productivity enhancement (Van Barneveld and Waring, 2002). Also pattern AWAs were very common, based on industry-based 'template' OEA agreements.

Using ABS data (ABS, 2004), Andrews (2005) claimed that workers on AWAs earned on average 13 percent more per week than workers on certified agreements and 100 percent more than workers on awards. In the December issue of the ADAM report, ACIRRT (2005:12–14) disaggregated the data by occupations and hours. Overall non-managerial employees on AWAs earned 2.1 percent less per hour than employees on collective agreements. Permanent part-time employees on individual contracts earned about 75 percent of those on collective agreements, with the corresponding ratio being 85 percent for casual employees, whereas full-time employees on individual contracts earned 2.1 percent more than employees on collective agreements. Women on AWAs were particularly disadvantaged.

ACIRRT (2005) compared a random sample of 500 AWAs which were certified in 2002 and provided by the OEA in 2004, with a sample of 591 federally certified enterprise agreements (207 non-union and 384 union agreements) from the ADAM database which were registered in 2002–2003. Employees on AWAs received an AAWI of 2.5 percent per annum, as compared to 4.3 percent under union collective agreements and 3.5 percent for non-union enterprise agreements. In addition, higher percentages of workers on AWAs were either not guaranteed a wage increase or were subject to 'at risk' wage increases involving performance reviews, meeting key performance indicators or employer discretion. A lower percentage of workers on AWAs were subject to wage increases linked to external measures (ACIRRT, 2005:13–14 and Table 2.3).

Wage Inequality

Between 1998 and 2004, the real weekly wages of the 80th percentile of adult non-managerial full-time employees grew 4.4 percent, whereas median real wage growth was 2.6 percent and the corresponding increase for the 20th percentile was 1.5 percent (ABS, 2004, 2005d). Real wage growth has accelerated since 2002, but at the cost of an increase in the disparity of real wage growth rates and hence higher wage inequality. Inequality is likely to widen further under the new WorkChoices legislation (Briggs, 2005).

Gender Wage Inequality

The Victorian Pay Equity Inquiry which was released in May 2005 found women working full-time were paid 18.4 percent less than their male counterparts. There was a 32 percent pay gap with respect to workers employed under individual agreements, which could worsen under WorkChoices. Twenty recommendations were made in the report, including the adoption of pay audits.

Executive Pay

The average base salary or 'come to work' pay increased 6 percent to $686,000 in 2005 for chief executives of the top 300 publicly listed Australian companies (AFR, 2005: S2), whereas in the year to September 2005 the increase for union and non-union newly certified agreements was 4 percent (DEWR, 2005a: 2). Taking account of bonuses and benefits the increase in executive remuneration was 11 percent (AFR, 2005: S2). Short term incentive bonuses increased 22 percent due to the strong profit performance. Average total remuneration for these executives rose 16 percent to $1.9 million ($5200 a day) which represented 34 times the average earnings of an adult full-time employee (Gittins, 2005).

AFR (2005: S2) reported that an average of 40 percent of total remuneration was still paid as fixed salary with a further 10 percent being paid in perks or other benefits, such as retention payments. Long term incentives, such as share options, were valued at 17 percent of the pay of the CEOs, but do not represent actual payments (AFR, 2005: S2). Retention payments or 'golden handcuffs' have attracted some criticism when not accompanied by performance hurdles (AFR, 2005: S4). Deals, sometimes in the form of consultancies, which prevent the CEO working for a rival company for a number of years, are increasing in frequency (AFR, 2005: S4).

Changes to corporate law required companies to prepare remuneration reports in 2005, which explained how pay policies reflected company policy over the previous four years. In particular, boards had to explain the criteria for the payment of bonuses, disclose the circumstances under which bonuses were not fully paid and outline company performance and shareholder returns (AFR, 2005: S4). Bonuses in some companies were discretionary, whereas, despite the existence of bonus policies, actual payments in some companies were discretionary, due to payment of other incentives in special circumstances. The AFR noted that earnings-per-share and other measures were often used to trigger bonuses, even though they did not always translate into higher share prices or dividends. Also such short-term measures were flawed because businesses were or should be operated with a longer term horizon.

In defence of high rates of remuneration, reference is often made to the world market for executives (Gittins, 2005), even though inconsistencies between company size, performance and executive remuneration were noted (AFR, 2005: S5; *The Western Australian*, 2005). At best, this suggests a poorly functioning market.

The Living Wage Case

Introduction

In late 2004 the Australian Council of Trade Unions (ACTU) filed its Living Wage Claim under the *Workplace Relations Act* 1996. The peak body requested a $26.60 per week increase in all award rates of pay with an equivalent increase in wage related allowances (AIRC, 2005a: para. 1). The Labor State and Territory Governments supported an increase of $20 per week in all minimum award rates (AIRC, 2005a: para. 21).

The Commonwealth argued for an $11 increase to minimum classification rates at or below the C10 classification in the Metal Industries Award (AIRC, 2005a: para. 15). The Commonwealth opposed the ACTU claim because they argued:

(a) it was inconsistent with the Act;
(b) it impeded employment for the low paid, low skilled and unemployed;
(c) it was poorly targeted with respect to assisting low-paid workers and inappropriate as a means of promoting social equity; and
(d) did not further the 'objects of the Act by encouraging agreement-making and promoting high levels of productivity' (AIRC, 2005a: paras. 15–16).

The major employer groups supported either a $10 or $11 per week increase, with some also advocating that the increase be confined to a limited number of award classifications. The groups cited a number of adverse economic consequences arising from the ACTU claim, including reduced economic security for the low paid, increased inflation due to insufficient productivity growth and rising interest rates, against the backdrop of the ongoing impact of drought (AIRC, 2005a: paras. 5–14).

Economic Background

There was a broad consensus that the economy had enjoyed moderate economic growth during 2004 (1.9 percent) and strong employment growth which saw the unemployment rate reach 5.1 percent in March 2005. Annual labour price index growth (3.6 percent) and price inflation (2.6 percent) were modest to December 2004. However productivity growth had declined due to a sharp growth in hours of 2.5 percent to December 2004 (AIRC, 2004: para. 17, paras 96–100).

The ACTU again relied on the relatively optimistic Treasury Mid-Year Economic and Fiscal Outlook forecasts to argue that their claim was affordable. Concern was expressed about the capacity of employers to absorb a 5.7 percent increase in the minimum wage in the absence of productivity improvements, when import costs were also rising. A number of medium-term risks were identified in submissions, with the Commonwealth and employer organizations providing a less optimistic perspective, but these risks were not directly associated with the granting of the claim.

The Commission engaged in a comprehensive analysis of economic data and forecasts (AIRC, 2005a: paras 148–156). They were sanguine about forecasts of slower output growth and found no evidence of a generalized acceleration of wage increases in the economy. They recognized that the impact of the ACTU's claim on overall earnings growth would be modest.

Legislative Requirements

The Commission noted that it had to take account of three categories of legislative obligation in determining the magnitude of the safety net adjustment (SNA), namely the economic impact with respect to employment, productivity and inflation; the social (need to provide fair minimum standards for employees, particularly the low paid, taking into account general community living standards); and the maintenance of the incentive to make enterprise agreements (AIRC, 2005a: paras. 157–158). No new substantive economic arguments to inform these issues were presented to the AIRC. We now consider each of the Commission's legislative obligations in turn.

Economic Impact

The Commission expressed concern at the lack of productivity growth over the previous 12 months, but noted that between June 1996 and March 2005 the CPI had remained within the RBA's target range of 2 to 3 percent per year for all but a few quarters (AIRC, 2005a: 10, para. 407).

The AIRC noted that the imposition of a minimum wage had the potential to reduce employment, but at the same time it conferred benefits (including reduced earnings inequality) which must be taken into consideration (AIRC, 2005a: 10, para. 410).

The 50 international studies about the impact on employment of a change in the minimum wage to which the Commonwealth referred had been considered in previous safety net review decisions (for example, see May 2004 decision, paras. 229–36). The Commission concluded that the 'research is either largely irrelevant, limited in scope or has serious methodological flaws' (AIRC, 2005a: 5.2, para. 17).

Specifically, studies by Leigh (2003) and Harding and Harding (2004) were considered to be 'methodologically flawed' (AIRC, 2005a: 5.4, para. 227). In addition, the technical assumptions underpinning the Monash study commissioned by the Commonwealth in 2005 was subject to a stringent critique by Mitchell (AIRC, 2005a: 5.3, paras. 202–220; Dixon, Madden and Rimmer, 2005; Mitchell, 2005b). In particular, the elasticities of labour demand (-0.63) and substitution between award and non-award labour (2.00) were not estimated. The Commission also pointed out that in the 2004 proceedings the Commonwealth relied upon the Harding and Harding study which estimated an elasticity of demand for labour of -0.21 percent, yet in the 2005 proceedings it relied on the Monash study which assumed an elasticity of -0.63 percent (AIRC, 2005a: 10, para. 409). The AIRC further argued that the ratio of the minimum wage and AWOTE for full-time adults had been in decline since 1996 (AIRC, 2005a: 5.4, para. 241). It noted that the minimum wage had been declining relative to bargained wages, the median wage and AWOTE since 1996, with higher Metal Industry award classifications declining even more against AWOTE (AIRC, 2005a: 10, para. 401 and Tables 20, 22). All classifications enjoyed real wage increases over the period from the June quarter 1996 to the March quarter 2004 with the C14 classification enjoying an increase of 10.5 percent and C6 0.4 percent, well below the real increase in AWOTE of 16.6 percent

The Commission also reported the equivocal conclusions of the June 1998 Employment Outlook (OECD, 1998) about the employment effects of minimum wages and concluded that there was

> a continuing controversy amongst academics and researchers about the employment effects of minimum wage improvements. There is nothing before the Commission to indicate that the controversy has been resolved. (AIRC, 2005a: 5.9, para. 279)

As in previous years the Commonwealth claimed that previous Safety Net increases had been to the detriment of employment in the award-reliant industries, despite evidence provided by the ACTU (AIRC, 2005a: 5.8, paras. 115, 118–120). The Commonwealth showed that there was a strong negative relationship between the annual change in employee hours worked in the three most award-reliant industries and the size of the Safety Net Adjustment of the Federal Minimum Wage (AIRC, 2005a: 5.8, Chart 13). This is a somewhat selective use of data. It would be customary to express both variables in percentage rather then absolute terms. Second, this 'strong' negative relationship is founded on seven observations and cannot be claimed to be robust. The type of econometric critique of the Commonwealth's evidence provided by Mitchell at the 2004 Safety Net case is again relevant (ACTU, 2004; AIRC, 2004: paras. 160–166).

The Commonwealth also argued that compositional changes in employment between award-reliant and agreement-based workers within each industry should be considered, although interpreting these changes is not straightforward. The Commission largely dismissed all evidence in this regard concluding that there was no necessary association between award coverage, safety net adjustments and employment growth (AIRC, 2005a: 5.8, para.278).

Wage Adjustment and the Propensity to Bargain

A number of submissions again explored the impact of the SNA on the willingness of the parties to bargain which must be considered by the Commission under Section 88A(d)(i) of the legislation. The AIRC noted that employers initiate bargaining and their failure to do so reflects in part the fact that the magnitude of the safety net increases had not provided them with sufficient incentive to do so (AIRC, 2005a: 6.1 para. 149).

The Commission noted the Commonwealth claim that safety net increases deterred the spread of enterprise bargaining, but itself highlighted the fact that in award-reliant industries, employment growth had been associated with enterprise bargaining. The Commission concluded that recent SNAs had been consistent with continued growth of bargaining in industries where award reliance was relatively high (AIRC, 2005a: 10, para. 417).

The Needs of the Low Paid

The Commission must 'ensure that a safety net of fair minimum wages and conditions of employment is ... maintained' (that is consider the matters specified in ss.88B(2)(a), (b) and (c)), but the needs of the low paid do not assume priority and will depend on prevailing circumstances (AIRC, 2005a: 7, para. 332).

The Australian Industry Group (AiG) argued that the needs of the low paid were better addressed through the broader social safety net rather than through minimum wages adjustments. The Commission agreed with the AiG and the Australian Catholic Commission for Employment Relations (ACCER) that if low paid employees gained (or lost) through the tax transfer system then, pursuant to s.88B(2)(c), the impact would be taken into consideration in the SNA, but a mechanistic approach would not be taken. The Commission considered that on balance income should be sourced from earnings rather than welfare (AIRC, 2005a: 7, para. 414).[2]

LaJeunesse, Mitchell and Watts (2006) argue that the annual adjustment of award minima has not been an act of charity, but rather is an appropriate means of ensuring relatively powerless workers participate in productivity growth, thereby preventing the creation of an underclass of working poor in Australia. It is curious that the Commonwealth and some employer organizations argue forcibly that family circumstances should inform the SNA, given that this principle is not applied to wage bargaining in general and does not appear in corresponding sections of the *Workplace Relations Act*.

The Commonwealth argued that SNA was poorly targeted because 42.8 percent of low-paid employees were in households with above median gross household income. HILDA data and other research showed that there was considerable upward mobility of income and earnings for low-paid workers (AIRC, 2005a: 7, para. 341). It claimed that for many Australians low-paid jobs enabled access to higher paid employment, so that the SNA should not lead to a major employment loss or inhibit the growth of new low-paid jobs (AIRC, 2005a: 7, para. 363).

However, the OECD (1996: 77) maintains that about two thirds of the cross sectional variance in annual earnings in six European countries and the USA reflected persistent differences in relative earnings. In a later study (OECD, 1997) persistent and recurrent low paid employment was found amongst women, older and less-educated workers. Also, countries with more deregulated labour and product markets did not appear to have higher relative mobility, nor did paid workers in these economies experience more upward mobility.

The Australian evidence on the mobility of low-paid workers is at best inconclusive. Burgess and Campbell (1998) and Dunlop (2000) fail to find a link between casual employment and permanent employment in Australia. Gaston and Timcke (1999) find some contrary evidence, but their study is confined to data from the Australian Youth Survey and is based on questionable econometric analysis.

The Commission agreed that bargained wage outcomes arising from agreements should not be transmitted through the award system and that the WPI was the most useful indicator of wage increases.

The Decision

On 7 June the Commission adjusted the safety net by $17 per week, raising the minimum wage by 3.6 percent to $484.40 and the tradesperson classification by 3 percent (AIRC, 2005a: 10, para. 424). The Commission rejected the proposal that the SNA should be confined to employees below the C10 classification, because of the significant erosion of the relativity since 1996 (AIRC, 2005a: 10, para. 425, Table 25).

Postscript

On Wednesday 21 December 2005 the Full Bench of the AIRC decided to adjourn the Safety New Review – Wages 2006 proceedings until the Australian Fair Pay Commission (AFPC) had made its first wage-setting determination in the Spring of 2006 (AIRC, 2005b).

Industrial Relations and Labour Market Reform

Bargaining Fees

The *Workplace Relations Amendment (Extended Prohibition of Compulsory Union Fees) Bill* 2005 was introduced into the House of Representatives on 9 March 2005 (Department of Parliamentary Services, 2005). It proposed to extend the prohibition on the inclusion of clauses in agreements relating to bargaining agents' fees beyond those certified under the *Workplace Relations Act* 1996 to also cover any state employment agreement to which a constitutional corporation is a party (p.7). A Bill had been introduced in 2004 following the decisions of the Western Australian and South Australian Commissions to allow the imposition of a bargaining agents' fees on non-union members (DiGirolamo, 2004; Workforce, 2004: 1438: 1, 8; Workforce, 2004, 1441: 2).

Superannuation Choice

Under the *Superannuation Legislation Amendment (Choice of Superannuation Funds) Act* 2004, employees engaged under a federal award were from 1 July 2005 able to select which super fund their employer should direct their 9 percent compulsory employer contribution (Fenech, 2005: 16). The legislation does not cover employees covered by a certified agreement, Australian Workplace Agreement, certain members of defined benefit schemes or a state award or industrial agreement, although legislation in some states also provide for the employee choosing her/his fund.

While promoting choice and apparently more intensive competition within the personal finance sector, this initiative relies for its effectiveness on the well informed consumer. The legislation ignores the significant costs to the employee of becoming better informed and follows initiatives in private health insurance where the patient can choose the best medical professional, and the increased consumer choice of pricing schemes of the utilities.

Family Provisions Case 2004 – the Work and Family Test Case

On 8 August 2005, the AIRC handed down its decision in the Family Provisions Test Case (AIRC, 2005c). The arguments presented by various parties were documented in Watts and Mitchell (2005). While all parties seemed to agree that greater flexibility in working arrangements was desirable, the ACTU and the employer groups disagreed on what flexibility meant or what form it should take.

Three new award provisions were granted (AIRC, 2005c: para. 396) such that an employee was given the right 'to extend the period of simultaneous unpaid parental leave ... up to a maximum of eight weeks' and 'to extend the period of unpaid parental leave ... by a further continuous period of leave not exceeding 12 months' and 'to return from a period of parental leave on a part-time basis until the child reaches school age.' The 'reasonable grounds' for refusal may 'include cost, lack of adequate replacement staff, loss of efficiency and the impact on customer service' (para. 396). All further unresolved claims in the case were referred back to a single commissioner for further conciliation.

The decision immediately inserted the test case standards into the 12 federal awards represented by the ACTU claim. The provisions do not apply to State awards or voluntary agreements. In the light of the WorkChoices legislation it is unlikely that the decision will spread in any significant way to other federal awards or place pressure on employers to include the provisions in negotiated agreements.

The Future of Wage Determination

The *Workplace Relations Amendment (Work Choices) Bill* 2005, (hereafter WorkChoices) was passed by both Houses of Parliament in December. The

AFPC will set and adjust the standard Federal Minimum Wage and minimum award classification rates of pay; special Federal Minimum Wages for junior employees, employees with disabilities or employees under training arrangements; minimum wages for piece workers; and casual loadings (House of Representatives, 2005: 11).

The 'no disadvantage test' in which an agreement was assessed on the basis of the relevant award has been replaced by the requirement that the agreement satisfy six statutory minimum standards – the Australian Fair Pay and Conditions Standard (AFPCS). The AFPCS specifies the minimum award wage, four leave entitlements (personal/carers, unpaid parental, compassionate and annual leave) and ordinary working hours. However ordinary working hours can be averaged over a year, enabling high weekly hours of work during peaks without overtime/penalty rates being paid. In addition, two weeks of annual leave can also be cashed out.

The Commonwealth Rationale for Change

The Commonwealth has argued that the AIRC safety net adjustments have retarded employment growth and the provision of apprenticeships and traineeships and that 'safety nets' should only apply to low paid workers (Howe et al., 2005: 4). Further, minimum wage determination should encourage labour market entry which is the stepping stone to higher paying jobs over time (Australian Government, 2005: 64). Without providing specific estimates, DEWR argued that the operation of the AFPC would benefit employment creation.

> DEWR has provided considerable evidence of the negative effects on employment arising from the operation of the current *Workplace Relations Act 1996* where the Australian Industrial Relations Commission (AIRC) continues to grant large wage rises in the annual Safety Net Review…The AFPC will ensure a better balance between fair pay and employment. (DEWR, 2005c: W319–06)

However, as reported in these reviews, the evidence provided by the Commonwealth and the major business lobby groups at Safety Net Hearings has been largely rejected by the AIRC. Watson (2004) presents a comprehensive survey and analysis of recent Australian and international studies of the relationship between changes in the minimum wage and employment and argues that no significant and consistent negative relationship between minimum wages movements and employment growth (or levels) has been found.

The proposition that wage increases adversely affect employment is grounded in orthodox microeconomic theory. Significant interdependencies between labour demand and supply are typically ignored by those who use 'text-book' theory as an 'authority' for their claims (Thurow, 1983).

The structure and proposed operation of the AFPC is documented in detail elsewhere (see Cowling and Mitchell, 2005). While the Commonwealth argues that the AFPC will be independent, the claim is compromised by the short-term nature of appointments and the Government's capacity to remain obedient to the selection criteria but appointing Commissioners sympathetic to its view about the need for slower real wages growth.

The Commonwealth wants 'a more consultative approach to minimum wage setting in Australia' (DEWR, 2005c: 20) and to move away from the 'legalistic and adversarial' process of minimum wage determination before the AIRC. However, the AIRC Safety Net decisions were based on the application of appropriate standards of evidentiary proof to the submissions of all parties (Briggs and Buchanan, 2005: 188) which were exacting and transparent. The Full Bench published a detailed evaluation and assessment of the evidence presented to explain the basis of its determination. Also it was recognized that specialized judicial processes were apposite in the case of labour relations (see also Mitchell, 2005a). Conversely, the AFPC will only need to publish its decisions with no legislative requirement for its processes or reasoning to be transparent.

Finally, unlike the AIRC (under Section 88B of the *Workplace Relations Act* 1996), the AFPC is not required to consider fairness in its decisions. Rather it must now only focus on four economic criteria (see House of Representatives, 2005: 49):

(a) The capacity of the unemployed and the low paid to remain in employment.
(b) employment and competitiveness across the economy;
(c) providing a safety net for the low paid; and
(d) providing minimum wages for junior employees, employees to whom training arrangements apply and employees with disabilities that ensure those employees are competitive in the labour market.

The Likely Effects

Wage Levels

Under WorkChoices nominal minimum and award classification wages will be protected at the level established by the 2005 Safety Net Review decision. The weekly Federal Minimum Wage cannot fall below $484.40, which translates to an hourly rate of $12.75 (House of Representatives, 2005: 19).

However, since the Federal Government's rationale for the creation of the AFPC is based on the view that the AIRC has been overly generous with respect to SNAs, future nominal minimum wage adjustments are likely to be smaller and less frequent. Accordingly, we expect the real minimum wage to fall over time or grow at a considerably slower rate. The adoption of (c) will lead to the narrowing of the cohort to which the decisions of the AFPC will apply.

DEWR (2005c: 14) states that the narrower focus of the AFPC reflects the Government's commitment to using the tax transfer system in conjunction with the workplace relations system to address the needs of the low paid. Howe et al. (2005: 4) argue that if the AFPC restricted real wages growth to the lowest classifications within a rationalized award structure the result would be 'a compression of award rates towards a de facto single minimum wage.'

Given economic criterion (d) noted earlier, it is likely that the AFPC will cut the real wages of the most disadvantaged, since persons aged 15–19 years and those with disabilities have high relative unemployment rates (8.3 percent in November 2003 and 16.3 percent in October 2005, respectively). We also note that in (c), the Government clearly wants to reduce the link between minimum wage adjustments and distributional equity, preferring a more coordinated approach via adjustments to wage, tax and transfer systems (House of Representatives, 2005). However, the chimera that the AFPC will focus exclusively on wage settings per se is belied by the fact that Government settings of rates and thresholds within the personal income tax system and the level, and targeting, of income support payments will impact on its decisions.

Briggs (2005:4–5) argues that low paid jobs will expand under WorkChoices via: (a) Award-dependent employees with low bargaining power will be transferred to low pay AWAs/non-union collective agreements by their employers who will exploit the minimum standards of the AFPC to avoid paying overtime/penalty rates and casual loadings; (b) Employees can be converted into contractors who are not covered by minimum labour standards and will have no recourse against exploitative arrangements; (c) New employees can be presented with 'take-it-or-leave-it' AWAs. Also the liberalized transmission of business[3], greenfield agreement[4] and unfair dismissal provisions will make these transitions easier; (d) Existing employees can be subjected to lower wages and reduced conditions of employment. Workplaces with terminated agreements will become permanently award-free and the WorkChoices legislation shifts the balance of power towards employers; (e) Employees working for corporations under state awards have no mechanism by which to achieve a wage increase during the three year transition period and will likely face a wage freeze.

In addition, even well-intentioned employers in cost-sensitive markets will face pressure to extract concessions from their workforce due to more intense wage competition from their less scrupulous competitors (LaJeunesse, Mitchell and Watts, 2006). Briggs (2005:6) notes that the legislation is complemented by tighter welfare to work reforms which will increase pressure on workers to accept poorly paid jobs, rather than suffer loss of benefits. The welfare reforms ensure a ready labour supply for these low paid jobs.

A number of other provisions in the Bill impact on the bargaining power of workers and hence their capacity to secure improvements in pay and conditions. These provisions include the exclusion of firms employing 100 and fewer employees from the Unfair Dismissal provisions, the limitations on strike action arising from the secret ballot provisions, the increased penalties for unlawful industrial action and the new powers for the Federal Minister to order protected industrial action to stop where the action threatens life, safety, health or welfare of the population or threatens significant damage to the economy. In addition, the right of entry of unions to workplaces are subject to greater restrictions.

Postscript

On 21 December the New South Wales Government announced that it was about to lodge a High Court challenge against the industrial relations changes. At the time of writing the Western Australian Government was in the final stages of preparing its High Court challenge (ABC, 2005).

Conclusion

During 2005 workers continued to enjoy modest wage increases, which have been augmented by changes in income tax rates and welfare entitlements. However, the rate of labour underutilization persists at high levels, which reflects the absence of a coherent full employment policy.

The future determination of wages and conditions has been profoundly changed by the passing of the WorkChoices Bill in December, which replaces union-oriented arbitration and conciliation processes with the operation of market forces, albeit within a highly regulated environment which strongly favours employers. The requirement that 'a safety net of fair minimum wages and conditions of employment be maintained' (*Workplace Relations Act*, 1996, s.88B(2)) has now been removed and replaced by a policy focused on employment and competitiveness, which is likely to become a low wage policy. LaJeunesse, Mitchell and Watts (2006) argue that unemployment is a macroeconomic phenomenon which signifies that the budget deficit is too low, rather than being the outcome of labour market inflexibility.

Notes

1 The wage cost index measures hourly wages net of bonuses and, in contrast to measures of average weekly ordinary time earnings (AWOTE), is independent of compositional changes, because it is based on a fixed basket of jobs, which, however, includes part-time jobs.

2 ACOSS also advocated reliance on minimum wages rather than transfers to stave off poverty (AIRC, 2005: 1, para.23).

3 Only current employees are bound by an existing agreement and only for one year if a business transfers its operations to a new entity.

4 Greenfield agreement regulations enable allow the employer to determine the terms and conditions for the first 12 months of a new business by making an 'agreement' with themselves (Briggs, 2005: 15).

Acknowledgement

Many thanks to Jenny Myers for her research assistance.

References

Andrews, K. (2005) '750,000 AWAs Approved', Media Release, 29 September http://mediacentre.dewr.gov.au/mediacentre/AllReleases/2005/September/750000AWAs Approved.htm

Australian Broadcasting Corporation (ABC) (2005) 'NSW Launches High Court Challenge to IR Laws', transcript of ABC news, 21 December.

Australian Bureau of Statistics (ABS) (2003) *Wage Cost Index, Australia*, Cat no. 6345.0, September. Canberra: ABS.

Australian Bureau of Statistics (ABS) (2004) *Survey of Employee Earnings and Hours*, Cat no. 6306.0, May 2004. Canberra: ABS.

Australian Bureau of Statistics (ABS) (2005a) *Labour Force, Australia*, Cat no. 6202.0, November 2005. Canberra: ABS.

Australian Bureau of Statistics (ABS) (2005b) *Average Weekly Earnings*, Cat no. 6302.0, August 2005. Canberra: ABS.

Australian Bureau of Statistics (ABS) (2005c) *Labour Price Index*, Cat no. 6345.0, September. Canberra: ABS.

Australian Bureau of Statistics (ABS) (2005d) *Consumer Price Index*, Cat no. 6401.0, September. Canberra: ABS.

Australian Centre for Industrial Relations Research and Training (ACIRRT) (2005) 'Agreements Database and Monitor (ADAM) Report', September and December.

Australian Council of Trade Unions (ACTU) (2004) 'ACTU Minimum Wage Case 2004 – Written Reply Submission', March.

AFR (2005) 'Executive Salaries', 16 November.

Australian Government (2005) *Work Choices: A New Workplace Relations System*, October, Commonwealth of Australia.

Australian Industrial Relations Commission (AIRC) (2004) 'Safety Net Review – Wages, May 2004', Decision PR002004.

Australian Industrial Relations Commission (AIRC) (2005a) 'Safety Net Review – Wages, 2005', Decision PR002005.

Australian Industrial Relations Commission (AIRC) (2005b) 'Safety Net Review – Wages, December 2005', Decision PR966840, http://www.airc.gov.au/fullbench/PR966840.htm

Australian Industrial Relations Commission (AIRC) (2005c) 'Family Provisions Case', Decision, http://www.airc.gov.au/fullbench/PR082005.htm#P1915_106588

Briggs, C. (2005) *Federal IR Reform – the Shape of Things to Come*, commissioned by Unions NSW, ACIRRT. Sydney: University of Sydney.

Briggs, C. and Buchanan, J. (2005) 'Work, Commerce and Law: A New Australian Model?', *Australian Economic Review* 38(2): 182–91.

Burgess, J. and Campbell, I. (1998) 'The Nature and Dimensions of Precarious Employment in Australia', *Labour and Industry* 8(3): 5–22.

Burgess, J. (1995) 'Aggregate Wage Indicators, Enterprise Bargaining and Recent Wage Increases', *Economic and Labour Relations Review* 6(2): 216–33.

Cowling, S. and Mitchell, W. F. (2005) 'Taking the Low Road: Minimum Wage Determination under "Work Choices", in G. Wrightson (ed.) *Creating a Culture of Full Employment*, pp. 196–206. Proceedings of the 7th Path to Full Employment Conference and the 12th National Unemployment Conference.

Department of Employment and Workplace Relations (DEWR) (2005a) 'Trends in Federal Enterprise Bargaining', September Quarter.

Department of Employment and Workplace Relations (DEWR) (2005b) 'Vacancy Report', accessed 15 December 2005 http://www.workplace.gov.au/workplace/Category/Publications/AgreementMaking/TrendsinFederal EnterpriseBargaining.htm

Department of Employment and Workplace Relations (DEWR) (2005c) 'Answer to Question on Notice W319–06, 2005–06 Budget Senate Estimates Hearing', Senate Employment, Workplace Relations and Education Legislation Committee, May.

Department of Parliamentary Services (2005) 'Workplace Relations Amendment (Extended Prohibition of Compulsory Union Fees) Bill 2005', Parliamentary Library Bills Digest Information, 138, Parliament of Australia http://www.aph.gov.au/library/pubs/BD/2004–05/05bd138.pdf

DiGirolamo, R. (2004) 'Non-union Workers Cop Bargaining Fee', *The Australian*, 15 April.

Dixon, P. B., Madden, J. R. and Rimmer, M. T. (2005) 'A Report to the Department of Employment and Workplace Relations', Centre of Policy Studies, Monash University.

Dunlop, Y. (2000) 'Labour Market Outcomes of Low Paid Adult Workers' (ABS Cat. No. 6293.0.00.005), Occasional Paper, Canberra: ABS.

EWRERC (2003) 'Bridging the skills divide', Employment, Workplace Relations and Education References Committee, Department of the Senate, Parliament House, Canberra.

Federal Coalition (2004) 'Flexibility and Productivity in the Workplace: The Key to Jobs', Federal Election Policy.

Fenech, A. (2005) 'Relief for Bosses as Workers Get Choosy', *The Australian*, 20 January: 16.

Gaston, N. and Timcke, D. (1999) 'Do Casual Workers Find Permanent Full-Time Employment? Evidence from the Australian Youth Survey', *Economic Record* 25(231): 333–47.

Gittins, R. (2005) 'Tough Times for CEOs: Making do on $5200 a day', *The Age*, 23 November: 2.

Gollan, P. (2000) 'Trends in Processes in the Making of Australian Workplace Agreements', Sydney: Office of the Employment Advocate.

Hawthorne, L. (2001) 'The Globalisation of the Nursing Workforce: Barriers Confronting Overseas Qualified Nurses in Australia', *Nursing Inquiry* 8(4): 213–29.

Harding, D. and Harding, G. (2004) 'Minimum Wages in Australia: An Analysis of the Impact on Small and Medium Sized Businesses', Report to the Department of Employment and Workplace Relations, March.

House of Representatives (2005) 'Workplace Relations Amendment (Work Choices) Bill 2005', Explanatory Memorandum, The Parliament of the Commonwealth of Australia, November.

Howe, J., Mitchell, R., Murray, J., O'Donnell, A. and Patmore, G. (2005) 'The Coalitions Proposed Industrial Relations Changes: an Interim Assessment', *Australian Bulletin of Labour* 31(3): 189–209.

LaJeunesse, R., Mitchell, W. F. and Watts, M. J. (2006) 'Economics and Industrial Relations: Debunking the Myths', in J. Teicher, R. Lambert and A. O'Rourke (eds) *WorkChoices: the New Industrial Relations Agenda*, pp. 123–41. Camberwell: Pearson Education Australia.

Leigh, A. (2003) 'Employment Effects of Minimum Wages: Evidence from a Quasi-Experiment', *The Australian Economic Review* 36(4): 361–73.

Mitchell, W. F. (2005a) 'Industrial Relations Changes: The Final Demise of a "Fair Go" Society!', *New Matilda*, May.

Mitchell, W. F. (2005b) 'Safety Net Review of Wages: Critique of Madden, Dixon and Rimmer', *Minimum Wages Case 2005*, Reply Composite Exhibit, R4.

Mitchell, W. F. and Quirk, V. (2005) 'Skill Shortages in Australia: Concepts and Reality', in G. Wrightson (ed.) *Creating a Culture of Full Employment*, pp. 307–323. Proceedings of the 7th Path to full Employment Conference and the 12th National Unemployment Conference.

Office of the Employment Advocate (OEA) (2005a) 'AWA Statistics: Who is making AWAs?', accessed 15 December 2005 http://www.oea.gov.au/graphics.asp?showdoc=/home/statistics.asp&SubMenu=2,

Office of the Employment Advocate (OEA) (2005b) 'AWA Fact Sheet', 30 November.

OECD (1996) 'The OECD Employment Outlook: Countering the Risks of Labour Market Exclusion', *OECD Observer*, Oct-Nov, Paris: OECD.

OECD (1997) *Implementing the OECD Jobs Strategy: Lessons From Member Countries' Experience*, OECD Publications Paris. http://www.oecd.org/sge/min/97study.htm

OECD (1998) *Employment Outlook*, June. Paris: OECD.

Reserve Bank of Australia (2005) 'Statement of Monetary Policy', Reserve Bank of Australia Bulletin, November.

Riley, J. and Sarina, T. (2006) 'Industrial Legislation in 2005', *Journal of Industrial Relations*, 48(3): 341–55.

The Western Australian (2005) 'Size no Barrier to Pay Rises', *The Western Australian*, 19 November: 76.

Thurow, L. (1983) *Dangerous Currents: The State of Economics*. Oxford: Oxford University Press.

Van Barneveld, K. and Waring, P. (2002) 'AWAs: A Review of the Literature and Debates', *Australian Bulletin of Labour* 28(2): 104–119.

Watson, I. (2004) 'Minimum Wages and Employment: A Comment', *Australian Economic Review* 37(2): 166–72.

Watts, M. J. and Mitchell, W. F. (2004) 'Wages and Wage Determination in 2003', *Journal of Industrial Relations* 46(2): 160–83.

Watts, M. J. and Mitchell, W. F. (2005) 'Wages and Wage Determination in 2004', *Journal of Industrial Relations* 47(2): 151–70.

Workforce (2004) Specialist Newsletters, Milsons Point, New South Wales.

4

Industrial Legislation in 2005

Joellen Riley
University of Sydney, Australia

Troy Sarina
University of Sydney, Australia

WorkChoices

The Howard government's second wave of industrial relations reforms proved to be a tsunami. In December 2005, this government used its effective control of the Senate to push through, in record time and some would say ill-considered haste, the most significant changes to Australia's system of industrial relations in the century since enactment of the *Conciliation and Arbitration Act* 1904 (Cth). The *Workplace Relations Amendment (Work Choices) Act* 2005 (WorkChoices) has all but paralysed the state industrial relations systems, destroyed the test-case system of determining basic wages and conditions of work by consultation with all stakeholders, gutted the system of arbitrated industry-based awards, withdrawn unfair dismissal protection from armies of Australian workers, and severely curtailed what little opportunity trade unions have to instigate industrial action in support of employees' claims. Those are the broad issues. The Act is also riddled with many little provisions which can only be explained as reactions to particular judicial decisions in favour of workers or unions which the government (or those who advised on the drafting of this legislation) did not like.

Given the magnitude of the WorkChoices changes, particularly the overriding of much state legislation, we may be forgiven in this year's review for ignoring state developments entirely, and focusing only on the overhaul of federal industrial laws.

Our usual commitment to keeping readers abreast of developments in discrimination law must also be set aside this year, under the imperative of dealing with considerably more momentous changes.

This report will attempt to overview in broad brush the major changes and their significance for employers, unions, workers and others with a stake in an effective system of industrial relations in Australia. We will not, in this necessarily brief report, be able to deal with the detail of the amendments. Detailed analysis will no doubt emerge over time, as the system's stakeholders begin to discover the full implications of these changes for their own enterprises. Whether WorkChoices will achieve its stated objective of invigorating productivity in the Australian economy remains to be seen. In the short term, it is certainly going to stimulate one sector of the economy: the market for legal advice.

A Death Knell for the State Systems?

The most significant effect of WorkChoices is that the federal system of industrial laws now overrides the States' systems. A new s. 16 of the *Workplace Relations Act* 1996 (Cth) (*WR Act*) provides that the *WR Act* applies to the exclusion of all State and Territory laws dealing with industrial relations, employment laws, pay equity, unfair dismissal and union rights of entry – with some notable exceptions. State anti-discrimination and equal opportunity statutes, and laws dealing with a list of 'non-excluded matters' will still apply to employers who are 'constitutional corporations' within the meaning of the federal statute. The non-excluded matters include occupational health and safety, long service leave, superannuation and some other matters. One particular victory in the fight to amend the original WorkChoices Bill to preserve some state protection for the most vulnerable of workers was the maintenance of the ethical clothing outworkers provisions in state legislation. Apart from occupational health and safety, however, the major aspects of industrial regulation – wage determination, basic conditions of work, enterprise bargaining, termination of employment – will be regulated exclusively by the federal system for all corporate employers. State systems will operate only where the federal system cannot. Unincorporated employers that have operated entirely within the state systems will continue to do so. Those who have been covered by federal awards and agreements will be covered by transitional provisions for up to five years, after which they must elect whether to incorporate and continue in the federal system, or rely instead on state regulation. Ironically, industrial regulation in Australia post WorkChoices is likely to remain a complex hybrid of federal and state regulation, despite the promises of a new national system, because of the peculiarities of the Australian Constitution, and because of the highly complex layered regulation introduced with WorkChoices. Stewart (2005: 210) has criticized the 'appalling complexity' which has made the *WR Act* 'unintelligible to all but experts'. It will be the unincorporated small business employers who will find the new system most confusing. Paradoxically, these often include the pastoralists who have been one of the principal constituencies that the Coalition government intended to benefit by these industrial reforms.

New Constitutional Underpinnings

Perhaps the most radical feature of WorkChoices is that it represents an abandonment of reliance on the labour power in s. 51(35) of the Australian Constitution to support federal industrial relations law. WorkChoices is underpinned principally by the corporations power in s. 51(20). This marks a fundamental shift in the form of regulation of industrial relations at the federal level. The traditional system of conciliation and arbitration of industry-wide awards depended upon the participation of a number of stakeholders – unions, employer bodies, state governments, social welfare organizations – to formulate standards for wage-setting and determination of basic working conditions, such as leave entitlements and reasonable working hours. Reliance on the corporations power allows the government to directly legislate to fix wages and conditions – so long as the employer is a 'constitutional corporation' – on the basis that the object of the legislation is to control or protect the activities of trading or financial corporations. Professor Ron McCallum has called this the 'corporatization' of Australian labour law, and has predicted that it will have far-reaching consequences for the way we think about labour law in Australia in the future (see McCallum, 2005).

Some of the States have indicated that they intend to mount a constitutional challenge to WorkChoices. The States are expected to argue that this legislation poses a significant threat to federalism by significantly undermining the ability of states to regulate economic activity within their borders. They are also likely to test the limits of the corporations power. The expansive interpretation that the High Court has already afforded the corporations power in other cases – notably the *Tasmanian Dam Case* (1983) 158 CLR 1 – weakens the States' prospects of success. The Keating government used the corporations power to underpin important elements of the *Industrial Relations Reform Act* 1993 (Cth). This legislation successfully withstood the Kennett Victorian government's challenge in all but some minor detail in *Victoria v Commonwealth* (1996) 187 CLR 416, although in that case, the parties conceded that the corporations power enabled federal regulation of the industrial rights and obligations of corporations. Indeed, the corporations power (assisted by the trade and commerce power in s. 51(1) and the Territories power in s.122) underpinned much of the *Workplace Relations and Other Legislation Amendment Act* 1996, including provisions in Part VIB for non-union collective bargaining, making Australian Workplace Agreements (AWAs), the freedom of association provisions in Part XA, and the unfair dismissal provisions. It is difficult to imagine that the High Court would declare these laws constitutionally invalid, but until the case is heard and decided, we can only speculate on its outcome.

A New Wage Fixing Body

Testimony to the abandonment of reliance on the labour power is the decision to replace the Australian Industrial Relations Commissions' (AIRC) award making role with a new wage fixing body – the Australian Fair Pay Commission (AFPC) – and a set of legislated minimum standards of work. The ACTU will no longer bring test cases to the AIRC for determination, after hearings at which all stakeholders make submissions. The AFPC is under no statutory obligation to hold any hearings at all, and may determine its own processes and procedures for fixing the Federal Minimum Wage (FMW) and Australian Pay and Classifications Scales (APCS) for workers. The other guaranteed basic working conditions include 'maximum ordinary hours of work' and minimum entitlements for annual leave, personal (sickness and carer's) leave, and parental leave. Much debate surrounded the hours of work standard. Although the legislation provides for a standard working week of 38 hours, this can be averaged over 12 months, and can be supplemented by a 'reasonable' number of additional hours requested by the employer. There is, consequently, no practically effective control on working time under these standards. Likewise, the guarantee of four weeks annual leave is illusory. The legislation provides that employers can request workers to cash out two of these weeks. Most significantly, these standards ignore the recommendations of the *Parental Leave Test Case 2005* (2005) 143 IR 245, and represent a step backwards in terms of progress towards work/family balance in standard Australian working conditions (Murray, 2005).

The Fate of Awards

No new federal awards can be made, because the AIRC has lost its powers to resolve industrial disputes by arbitration. Existing awards will be maintained (so long as the employer is a constitutional corporation) until the employer and employees enter into workplace agreements. However these awards will contain only 13 (not 20) allowable award matters: s. 513. Allowable award matters include such matters as redundancy pay (but only for employers with more than 15 employees), stand down provisions and dispute settling procedures. A new s. 515 lists matters which are specifically *not* allowable in awards, including union representation rights, trade union training leave, rights for long term casuals to move from casual to permanent work, minimum and maximum hours for part time work, staffing levels, the use of contractors and labour hire, tallies and union picnic days. Many of these matters represent old industrial battles, now won conclusively for the employers (at least while the Work Choices laws remain on the statute books).

The matters covered by the Australian Fair Pay and Conditions Standards (AFPCS), except for ordinary working hours, are not allowable award matters: s. 516. However it is possible that an old award provision which is more generous than the AFPCS may continue to apply to a particular employee because they are 'preserved award terms': see ss 527 to 533. The preservation of certain award terms is an attempt to meet the government's political commitment that no worker should be disadvantaged – at least in basic conditions of work – by the enactment of WorkChoices. (This commitment of course discounts the more subtle disadvantages that workers face by the loss of many collective industrial rights.)

The preserved award conditions will survive the rationalization of an award, but they cannot be extended to new employers who have agreed to be covered by an award, nor to new classes of employees. Employers currently operating under state awards may opt into the federal system by applying to become bound by a relevant federal award: see ss 557 and following.

Employers Under State Awards and Agreements

Schedule 15 of WorkChoices makes provision for State registered enterprise agreements to continue in force until they are terminated voluntarily, until they reach their nominal expiry date, or on a date three years from their commencement, whichever is sooner. So long as the employer is a constitutional corporation, these 'preserved state agreements' will be enforced in the federal system as federal workplace agreements. These employers will no longer have any recourse to state industrial tribunals for dispute resolution. Any provisions in preserved state agreements which are 'prohibited content' (see later in the discussion of workplace bargaining) or offend any other *WR Act* requirement will be invalid and unenforceable.

Preserved state agreements will terminate on the making of a federal workplace agreement, or if the AIRC makes a 'workplace determination', which – like the old s. 170MX awards – can be made if the AIRC terminates a bargaining period under the new s. 430 because the parties have failed to genuinely try to reach agreement, or their dispute is causing economic harm or threatens safety. Once a workplace agreement or workplace determination is made, the state agreement cannot be revived. Parties who are bound by a current preserved state agreement will not be able to take protected action when negotiating for a federal workplace agreement.

Corporate employers who have been operating on state awards prior to WorkChoices will continue to be bound by those state awards, which have transformed into 'notional agreements preserving state awards'. These can last for three years from the commencement of WorkChoices, but may also terminate earlier if the parties negotiate a federal workplace agreement. Any award terms which are non-allowable, prohibited, or offend any other provision of the *WR Act* will be unenforceable. For example, the union rights of entry provisions typically allowed in many state awards will be void.

Unincorporated Employers on Federal Awards

Transitional provisions allow employers who are not incorporated but who have operated until now on federal awards to continue to use those awards, subject to rationalization of the awards down to the 13 allowable matters, for a maximum of five years. Beyond that time, such employers will need to decide whether to opt into the federal system by incorporating, or to take their chances with regulation under what remains of the State industrial relations systems.

Of course, in the absence of any valid federal or state regulation, the common law of employment will apply to their relationships with their workers (Riley, 2005).

Workplace Bargaining

WorkChoices has also reformed the process of agreement making. In accordance with the objective of 'enabling employers and employees to choose the most appropriate form of agreement for their circumstances'(*WR Act*, s. 3(e)), provisions pertaining to AWAs and collective agreements have now been combined in a new Part 8 of the Act. In line with the Coalition's emphasis on individual agreement making, regulation of AWAs is given primacy under this section. The reform package also provides for employer greenfields agreements: s. 330. This new form of agreement allows the employer of a new enterprise to make an agreement with itself, *without* seeking the approval of employees before lodging the agreement for approval. However, the most significant aspects of the legislation are amendments to both the *procedural* and *substantive* aspects of agreement making. These changes raise serious doubts as to whether this new regulatory framework will achieve its objectives of 'higher productivity' and the creation of a 'fair labour market': s. 3(a).

One of the most significant changes to the agreement making process is the removal of obligations placed on employers to *inform* employees of their rights to union representation. Section 335 provides that employees who will be subject to a collective agreement 'may request another person to represent the employee in meeting and conferring with the employer': s. 335(1). This assumes that employees are aware of their rights to representation. This may be true in highly unionized workplaces, but is unlikely to be the case in those workplaces with little or no union presence. In *Re Application by AFMEPKIU in relation to breach of s. 170MW; Morris McMahon & Co Pty Ltd & Automotive, Food, Metals, Engineering, Printing and Kindred Industries Union*, PR931192, Sydney, 8th May 2003 at 7, Munro J noted that many employers pursue the formation of non-union collective agreements as it allows them to assert their own choice of employee bargaining unit, providing them with a greater degree of control over the negotiation process. Former s. 170LK had acknowledged the importance of ensuring employees were aware of their rights to representation. Under s. 170MW(4), the employer was under an obligation to inform *any* person who was a member of a union of their right to representation. This obligation has now been removed.

There has also been a significant reduction in employers' obligations to provide information about any proposed agreement. Under s. 339(1)(a) and (2), the employer is only required to provide employees with *access* to the agreement seven days before it is submitted for approval. This period has been reduced from the 14 days required under former ss 170LJ and 170LK, limiting employees' opportunity to scrutinize any proposal. However, the most concerning aspect of these reforms is the removal of the obligation imposed by former ss

170LJ(3)(b) and 170LK(7) that the employer take reasonable steps to *explain* the terms of the agreement to employees. Now, the employer is only required to provide an *information statement* about the agreement. Sections 337(4)(a–d) provide that the only mandatory information to be conveyed in this statement is the time when agreement will be submitted for approval and that nominated bargaining agents have been given an opportunity to meet and confer with the employer. Providing any further information regarding the actual *content* of the agreement is up to the discretion of the approving body, the Office of the Employment Advocate (OEA), who is obliged to publish its requirements in the Industrial Gazette: s. 337(4). Furthermore, s. 338 allows employees to waive their right to this information statement in order to speed up the approval process. Section 342 also attempts to speed up the process of agreement making by requiring the agreement to be submitted for application within 14 days of being approved by employees. This submission period has been reduced from 21 days under former s. 170LM. It is difficult to see how these changes will facilitate parties being able to effectively determine which industrial instrument is most appropriate to regulate their conditions of employment. Section 347(2) provides that if an agreement passes the scrutiny of the OEA and is certified *without* meeting the procedural requirements relating to information obligations, the agreement is still deemed to come into operation, in effect enabling employers to circumvent the procedural requirements if they choose to do so.

One beneficial amendment to the agreement making procedures relates to the additional requirements for approving AWAs that cover employees who are under the age of 18. Section 340 states that before such an AWA is approved it needs to be 'signed and dated by an appropriate person' such as the employee's parent or guardian in order to signify there has been genuine consent to making of such an agreement. This amendment targets the contractual difficulties associated with this type of industrial agreement. Considering that AWAs rely on the fundamental contract principles of offer and acceptance, consideration, certainty and an intention to be bound (Fetter and Mitchell, 2004: 4), there is considerable debate surrounding the capacity of a person under the age of 18 years to be legally competent to enter into such an arrangement. Section 340 attempts to safeguard against accusations that employees under the age of 18 have been exploited.

There have also been a number of amendments affecting the substantive fairness of agreement making. One of the most significant is the removal of the no disadvantage test (NDT) in former Part VIE, which ensured that employees were, *overall*, no worse off under the proposed agreement than the minimum conditions prescribed by a relevant award: former ss 170X–170XF. Section 344(5) states that the Employment Advocate is *not* required to examine the content of the workplace agreement, effectively removing the main statutory mechanism for ensuring equitable considerations 'would not be forgotten in the new decentralised system' (see Waring and Lewer, 2001: 66). Although the NDT was not without its faults as an effective safeguard of employee conditions, it still provided some degree of protection for employees in the quest for productivity gains through increased workplace flexibility.

The approach to regulating the content of agreements outlined in ss 353 and 354 is also of grave concern. Section 352(b)(i) states that workplace agreements can now have a term of five years, so employees' opportunity to renegotiate agreements, and take protected industrial action in support of claims, is limited to every five years. Although there have been suggestions that the shift towards enterprise-based bargaining has led to both parties being 'bargained out' by the requirement to renew agreements every three years (see Campling and Gollan, 1999), the ability for parties to effectively predict the appropriate conditions of employment for a whole five year term can only be characterized as problematic. If the government wished to construct an industrial relations system to accommodate a 'flexible' labour market as well as rapid changes in the domestic and global economy, implementing a rigid process of agreement making that binds parties for half a decade seems somewhat contradictory.

Prohibited Content

One of the most contentious changes to agreement making concerns the Coalition's attempt to deal with the issue of what matters pertaining to the employment relationship should be able to be included in registered workplace bargains. In *Electrolux Home Products Pty Ltd v AWU* (*Electrolux*) (2004) 78 ALJR 1231, the High Court held that the inclusion of claim for a union bargaining agents fee in a proposed enterprise agreement meant that the proposed agreement was not certifiable, and any action taken in support of it could not be protected action. WorkChoices expressly prohibits bargaining agents fees: s. 801. However, *Electrolux* did not provide an exhaustive list of matters that did pertain to the employment relationship. This has resulted in a great deal of uncertainty about the validity of provisions in agreements that refer to contract labour, union facilities and salary sacrificing (Creighton and Stewart, 2005: 212–213). Consequently, a new s. 356 attempts to resolve the issue by providing that the Minister may table Regulations specifying matters that are prohibited. A set of Regulations prohibiting a long list of matters was released on 19 March 2006: see Workplace Relations Regs 8.5 to 8.7. No doubt the government and the employer involved in the *Electrolux* matter experienced some frustration at the lengthy litigious process involved in settling this question. It is indeed more expeditious to allow a Minister to make up the rules, ad hoc, as contentious issues emerge – but this approach offends the rule of law. The objects of legal regulation ought to be able to organize their affairs with knowledge of their legal obligations. Empowering the Minister with an unfettered discretion to blow the whistle on the game and change the rules – without any Parliamentary scrutiny of those changes – it highly unsatisfactory, especially as the enforcement of this prohibition on certain content is to be so heavy-handed. Seeking to include prohibited content in an agreement will attract civil penalties of up to $33,000: s. 357(3). The ministerial discretion to shift the goal posts calls into question whether any registered workplace agreement will in fact represent the parties' own 'work choices'. The OEA must remove any prohibited content from an agreement, even if the agreement has already been approved: s. 359. In effect, this could mean that parties who have negotiated a five year agreement, may later be informed that a number of elements that were essential to reaching such an agreement have now been removed, so that they are obliged to operate under an agreement that does not reflect the trade-offs that the parties initially agreed upon. Indeed, many of the so-called reforms to agreement making are difficult to reconcile with a number of the purported objectives of WorkChoices. It is hard to see how these changes – described by Senator Andrew Murray during the Senate debate as 'authoritarian micromanagement' of Australian workplaces – will facilitate simplified agreement making and fostering more collaborative relationships between employers and employees.

Controls on Industrial Action

The ability of unions to undertake industrial action to support bargaining has also been seriously curtailed by WorkChoices. No protected action can be taken in support of a workplace agreement until an elaborate secret ballot process has been followed: ss 109ff. Ostensibly these procedures are intended to ensure that an unrepresentative minority of activists is not able to initiate industrial disruption. This view – that most of the work force are happy and compliant and only a fractious minority cause industrial strife – has been shown to be unsubstantiated by research in the past (McCallum, 1975).

Not only will it be harder to take protected action, unprotected action will also be more susceptible to legal sanction. A new s. 496 (replacing former s. 127), provides that if the AIRC becomes aware that any unprotected industrial action is happening it must issue an order that it stop. The discretion afforded by the word 'may' meant that employers were occasionally refused applications in the past: see *Coal and Allied Operations Pty Ltd v Amalgamated Metals Union* (1997) 73 IR 311. The slight brake on employers taking precipitate tort actions against unions and workers provided by former s.166A has now been repealed. Employers no longer have to wait 72 hours while the AIRC attempts to resolve a matter before litigating. Whether employers will see any benefit in rushing off to court with writs to antagonize their workforces remains to be seen. The extraordinarily low level of litigation for industrial torts over the past century tends to suggest that most employers see no commercial or industrial advantage in suing their workers.

Dispute Resolution

WorkChoices has reduced the dispute resolution powers of the AIRC, and encourages parties to engage alternative dispute resolution (ADR) avenues.

Under s. 353 all agreements must include a dispute resolution procedure. If the parties fail to agree on their own dispute resolution procedure, the model dispute resolution process in Part 13 of the Act is deemed to apply. These amendments have dramatically changed the general role of the AIRC in relation to dispute resolution. Under s. 698, the Commission can assist in facilitating a range of dispute resolution methods including conferencing, mediation and even assisting in negotiations – all activities already authorized under former s. 111 of the *WR Act*. The major difference, however, is that although the Commission has power to facilitate these activities it does *not* have the power to 'compel a person to do anything or arbitrate on a matter or make an order' in relation to these activities: s. 701(5). The Commission does not have the power to make orders in relation to disputes over the terms of an agreement *unless* this power has been given to it via the terms of an agreement reached. This effectively removes the power of the Commission to intervene in agreement making *unless* sanctioned by both parties. However, there do seem to be some alternative avenues for ensuring that the Commission's role in agreement making is not completely removed. Under s. 430, the Commission retains the power to make an order to suspend or terminate a bargaining period if it can ascertain that one party has not made an attempt to 'genuinely bargain' to reach an agreement. This is a revamped version of s. 170MW used by the Commission in the past to imply an obligation to bargain in good faith into the *WR Act*. This can only assist in ensuring that both parties have enforceable obligations when negotiating for an agreement (Lee, 2004: 5).

Union Rights of Entry

WorkChoices also restricts union entry and inspection rights. The objectives in s. 736 state that this regulatory system intends to allow 'employers to conduct their business without undue interference or harassment' and to ensure that permit holders are 'fit and proper' persons. This is a significant departure from former s. 285A of the *WR Act* which allowed union officials to be issued with right of entry permits *without* having to meet such a test. Section 285A(3) allowed an industrial registrar to revoke this permit, if the person had acted in an 'improper manner'. Under WorkChoices the assumption that any person is eligible to hold a permit has been removed. The provisions indicate how this fit and proper person test can be met by listing the circumstances in which a permit is *not* to be issued. Issues that need to be considered include: whether the official has had appropriate training about the rights associated with holding a permit, whether the applicant has ever been convicted of an offence against an industrial law or any other Federal or State law, and whether the person has ever had a permit revoked: s. 742(2)(a)–(h). It is unclear whether a person is automatically deemed to be a 'fit and reasonable person' as long as s. 203 does not apply. It is difficult to reconcile the government's sense of urgency in reforming right of entry regulations with the fact that the AIRC has had to hear only one matter relating to union inspections (AIRC in 2004–2005).[1] Section

754 has also reversed the burden of proof that is required for a permit holder to exercise a right of entry. Under former s. 285B there was an assumption that a breach had occurred until proven otherwise. Under the new provisions, a permit holder now needs to provide a detailed explanation of *why* they should be granted a right of entry.

WorkChoices also changes the rights of permit holders to enter the workplace for the purpose of holding discussions with employees. These amendments highlight the resurgence of managerial prerogative in this area. For example, the requirements for an employer to obtain a conscientious objection certificate, which effectively prohibits unions from entering the workplace on religious grounds, have been made easier. Under former s. 285C employers could apply for such certificates as long as *all employees* had agreed that the employer's application should be endorsed. New s. 762 allows employers to make this application in their own right.

Section 765 has made it more difficult for a union to claim that an employer has refused to comply with a request to enter the workplace. Section 765(2) states that a permit holder is not authorized to enter the workplace without demonstrating compliance with 'reasonable' requests by the employer to adhere to occupational health and safety standards and to hold discussions in a particular area or room. These provisions seems to be a direct response to cases such as *ANZ Banking Group v Finance Sector Union of Australia* PR 951766 (Melbourne, 8 September 2004) which involved a dispute over whether a permit holder's right to interview employees under former s. 285B (3) (c) of the *WR Act* allowed a union official to walk through a worksite and approach employees at their workstations to discuss joining the union. Section 765(4) now allows employers a prerogative to set the time and place of union discussions. An employer can require union officials to use a particular room for interviews or take a particular route to hold discussions whilst at the workplace. Unions may not claim that such directions are 'unreasonable'.

There are now additional requirements for union officials who wish to enter workplaces to ensure compliance with Occupational Health and Safety (OHS) regulations. Section 756 states that any person wishing to investigate a breach must have met the right of entry requirements outlined earlier *even* if they have already been issued a right of entry permit under state OHS laws. Also, s. 758 significantly alters the obligations that such permit holders have under state laws. For example, under s. 77 of the *Occupational Health and Safety Act* (NSW) (2001) (*OHS Act*), union officials hold a presumption of entry allowing them to inspect a worksite conditional upon meeting notification requirements prescribed by the *OHS Act*. However, under s. 758 of the *WR Act*, an employer can now refuse entry to an official if they refuse to comply with a 'reasonable' request for officials to adhere to OHS guidelines that govern the workplace. However there is little detail in the provisions to assist parties to identify what constitutes a 'reasonable' request. The culmination of these changes is a removal of any implied right that unions previously had to enter the workplace. Unions now face a new obligation to justify why they should be afforded the opportunity to enter. Again, these restrictions seem ironic considering that the WorkChoices changes ostensibly encourage parties not only to set their conditions of employment but also to determine the appropriate mechanisms for enforcing these conditions. By restricting union rights of entry, these amendments have effectively placed further constraints on the ways parties can choose to regulate compliance with both agreement conditions and OHS standards.

The Building and Construction Industry

The *Building and Construction Industry Improvement Act* 2005 (Cth) *(BCII)* is the government's response to the Cole Royal Commission into the Building and Construction Industry which presented its findings to Parliament in 2003. This new Act has implemented a number of initiatives aimed at stamping out alleged corruption within the building industry. Part 1 of the Act establishes the Australian, Building and Construction Commissioner (ABC) which is a new body that is responsible for a range of activities including 'monitoring and promoting appropriate standards of conduct for building industry participants' and providing general assistance and advice. The ABC can initiate action against an employer to ensure that employee entitlements are protected as well as having the power to share information with other regulatory bodies to deal with issues ranging from tax evasion, the collection of workers compensation premiums and the concealment of funds in shelf companies, subject to limitation in *BCII* s. 65.

The more contentious functions of the ABC have prompted union accusations that the BCII represents an ideologically driven campaign to eradicate unions. Section 43 allows the ABC to take action on behalf of anyone who has been victimized or coerced by a person in an attempt to gain employment or secure a contract. The federal secretary of the CFMEU, David Noonan (2005:11), has expressed the view that this new raft of regulations is the result of an ideological witch hunt, considering that the $66 million Royal Commission only resulted in one isolated prosecution due to coercion. In Noonan's view, enacting a statute with the primary purpose of scrutinizing the activities of industrial organizations represents an 'unbalanced approach' to regulating the industry. Noonan claims a vast number of award and agreement breaches by employers are ignored. Further, s. 52 allows the ABC to compel individuals to provide information pertaining to an investigation. Failure to comply with these requests is a criminal offence, so that employees may be jailed if they refuse to 'dob on [their] workmates' (Noonan, 2005: 11).

The other major element of the *BCII* that has generated widespread controversy is s. 36 which provides for civil penalties for a range of activities deemed to be 'unlawful industrial action'. These include delayed performance of building work in relation to an industrial dispute, and the failure of employees to perform work while at the worksite, except where there is 'an imminent risk to his or her health and safety': s 36(g)(i). Section 27 also allows the Minister to issue a 'Building Code' outlining the conditions attached to certain projects.

Some recent decisions by the AIRC highlight the extensive powers of the ABC. In a decision involving a rail project in Western Australia, the AIRC issued Leighton Constructions with a former s. 127 order banning the CFMEU from taking industrial action after Commissioner John Lloyd from the ABC intervened in the proceedings. Such intervention is allowed under s. 72 of the *BCII*. In *Leighton Kumagai Joint Venture*, PR966077, 6 December 2005, the AIRC held that the CFMEU had failed to the follow the dispute resolution procedure in the agreement that covered this project by engaging in industrial action and as a consequence had failed to display the 'greater level of flexibility' required under s. 36 of the *BCII*. The workplace agreement allowed for employees to work up to 56 hours a week, but the CFMEU had not complied with this provision as they believed that the employees had been working too hard. Previously, such actions would have been categorized as simple breaches of the agreement resulting in non-payment. However, since this failure to work the agreed hours provided in the agreement could be classified as a 'ban', the CFMEU and its members *could* be classified as engaging in 'unlawful' industrial action as defined under the *BCII*. In a period of industrial reform that is aimed at facilitating a further shift towards a decentralized model or regulation, the *BCII* advocates a highly interventionist approach to regulating an essential industry in the Australian economy. It is difficult to see that regulation which promotes antagonism between the parties will foster the co-operative relationships required to generate sustained economic growth.

Termination of Employment

Employees who work for a corporation which employs 100 or fewer employees will no longer be able to bring any proceedings before an industrial tribunal – state or federal – in pursuit of remedies for unfair dismissal: s. 643(10). The head count includes all permanent employees and casuals who have been engaged on a regular and systematic basis for at least 12 months. Concerns that unscrupulous employers might seek to exploit this threshold by carving their workforces up into parcels of less than 100 workers, and engaging them among a number of separate subsidiaries were addressed by a late amendment to the WorkChoices bill that included the employees of any related bodies corporate in the head count: s. 643(11). Even very large enterprises will be able to dismiss workers without the risk of unfair dismissal proceedings if they can justify those dismissals on the basis that 'genuine operational reasons' were among the reasons for selecting the employee for dismissal: s. 643(8). 'Operational reasons' has been defined broadly to include any reason of an 'economic, technological, structural or similar nature': s. 643(9). The government has continued to assert that these changes are necessary to stimulate employment growth. As Stewart (2005: 210) notes (citing Barrett, 2005; Robbins and Voll, 2004 and Waring and de Ruyter, 1999), empirical studies have proven no link between the availability of unfair dismissal protection and employer hiring practices.

Unlawful dismissal protection remains for all employees, regardless of the size of the enterprise. It has been suggested in a number of informal public forums that the continuing availability of unlawful dismissal protection to small business employees may stimulate a rise in the number of claims of discriminatory dismissals. Time alone will tell.

Transmission of Business

A new Part 11 deals with the obligations of employers who acquire businesses, or parts of businesses, from former employers who have been bound by industrial instruments. Whereas the old transmission of business rules caused the provisions of an industrial award or agreement to be carried across to a new business owner, regardless of whether the new employer engaged the old employees, the new rules will apply only if the new business owner employs at least one 'transferring employee'. It appears that a straightforward way of avoiding the application of any transmission of agreements would be to refuse to engage any of the existing staff of the business. If a new employer does take on the old staff, then the terms and conditions of any workplace agreement binding on the old employer will also bind the new employer – but only in respect of transferring employees (s. 585(5)), and only for a 'transmission period' of a maximum of 12 months: s. 580(4). Similarly, a transmitted award is only binding in respect of transferring employees for a period of 12 months: see s. 595.

Conclusions

There is a great deal more in the detail of the *WorkChoices* changes. Only time – and (we predict) considerable industrial turmoil – will tell whether this radical reconfiguration of Australian industrial laws will deliver on the government's promises of greater economic prosperity in Australia over the long term.

Notes

1   For more information see the Annual Report of the President of the Australian Industrial Relations Commission and the Annual Report Of The Australian Industrial Registry, 1st July 2004 to 30th June 2005: 64.

References

Barrett, R. (2005) 'Small Business and Unfair Dismissal', The Federal Government's Industrial Relations Policy: Report Card on the Proposed Changes, University of Sydney.

Campling, J. and Gollan, P. (1999) *Bargained Out*. Sydney: Federation Press.

Creighton, B. and Stewart, A. (2005) *Labour Law*. Sydney: Federation Press.

Fetter, J. and Mitchell, R. (2004) 'The Legal Complexity of Workplace Regulation and its Impact upon Functional Flexibility in Australian Workplaces', Working Paper No.31, Centre for Employment and Labour Relations Law, September 2004.

Lee, M. (2004) 'Bargaining in Good Faith, Coercion and Duress: Relative Flexibility in the Twenty-First Century' presented at the Australian Labour Law Association Second

National Conference: Employment Regulation for the Changing Workplace, 24th–25th September, Faculty of Law, University of Sydney.

McCallum, R. (1975) 'The Mystique of Secret Ballots: Labour Relations Progress v Industrial Anarchy', *Monash University Law Review* 2: 166–79.

McCallum, R. (2005) 'Justice at Work: Industrial Citizenship and the Corporatisation of Australian Labour Law', Kingley Laffer Memorial Lecture, University of Sydney, 11 April 2005.

Murray, J. (2005) 'The AIRC's Test Case on Work and Family Provisions: The End of Dynamic Regulatory Change at the Federal Level?', *Australian Journal of Labour Law* 18(3): 325–43.

Noonan, D. (2005) 'The ABCC: Industrial umpire or union buster?' CCH *Industrial Law News* 10: 24 October.

Riley, J. (2005) *Employee Protection at Common Law*. Sydney: Federation Press.

Robbins, W. M. and Voll, G. (2004) 'Who's Being Unfair? A Survey of the Impact of Unfair Dismissal Laws on Small Regional Businesses' 18th AIRAANZ Conference, Noosa.

Stewart, A. (2005) 'A Simple Plan for Reform? The problem of Complexity in Workplace Regulation', *Australian Bulletin of Labour* 31(3): 210–36.

Waring, P. and Lewer, J. (2001) 'The No Disadvantage Test Failing Workers', *Labour and Industry* 12(1): 65–86.

Waring, P. and de Ruyter, A. (1999) 'Dismissing the Unfair Dismissal Myth', *Australian Bulletin of Labour* 25(3): 251–74.

5

Major Tribunal Decisions in 2005

Joseph Catanzariti
Clayton Utz, Australia

Michael Byrnes
Clayton Utz, Australia

Introduction

The introduction of the Federal Government's WorkChoices reforms is set to change, in a fundamental way, much of the very basic foundations of Australian labour law. Despite the passage of these significant new amendments, several areas of established Australian labour law will continue to be relevant. A number of important judicial decisions of the last 12 months highlight the areas in which the law is likely to develop. This article reviews key 2005 decisions relating to the meaning of 'reinstatement' in unfair dismissal cases, the Family Test Case, the liability of managers under occupational health and safety laws and the relief available in workplace bullying cases.

The Meaning of Reinstatement

The Australian Industrial Relations Commission (AIRC) is empowered under s.170CH (now s. 654) of the *Workplace Relations Act* 1996 (Cth) (WRA) to make several orders if it finds that an employee has been unfairly dismissed.[1] Such orders include an order requiring the employer to reinstate the dismissed employee (s. 170CH(3)(a) of the *WRA*; now s. 654(3)). In *Blackadder v Ramsey Butchering Services Pty Ltd*[2] the High Court was called upon to clarify exactly what such an order of reinstatement involves.

Mr Blackadder had been employed by Ramsey Butchering Services Pty Ltd as a 'boner' and was required to work in the 'boning rooms' where he performed work on pre-chilled pieces of beef carcases. On 28 September 1999, Ramsey directed Mr Blackadder to perform work on the 'slaughter floor' where he was required to perform 'hot neck boning work'. Mr Blackadder refused to perform this work on the grounds that he had no prior experience or training in such work and that in performing the duties he might aggravate a pre-existing injury to his right elbow. Ramsey terminated Mr Blackadder's employment for refusing to perform duties as directed. Mr Blackadder subsequently commenced unfair dismissal proceedings under the WRA. The AIRC found in Mr Blackadder's favour and made an order for his reinstatement.[3]

Following an unsuccessful appeal of the AIRC's decision,[4] Ramsey agreed to reinstate Mr Blackadder to his position as a boner and to pay his average weekly remuneration, but refused to allow him to physically return to work until he submitted to a medical examination. Mr Blackadder refused to attend the medical examination, claiming that the AIRC's order was not conditional upon it, and that he was ready, willing and able to resume his work as a boner. Mr Blackadder and Ramsey continued to contest their respective positions until Mr Blackadder applied to the Federal Court seeking enforcement of the AIRC's order.

At first instance, Justice Madgwick of the Federal Court made a declaration that Ramsey had breached the AIRC's order.[5] Specifically, Justice Madgwick ordered that Mr Blackadder be reinstated to his former position, namely 'a boner performing chilled boning work in that part of the respondent's premises known as the big boning room'. Ramsey subsequently appealed to the Full Court of the Federal Court, and a majority of that Court partially allowed the appeal.[6] In allowing parts of Ramsey's appeal, the majority of the Full Court relied upon the common law position, which holds that an employer has no obligation to provide work to an employee, unless the contract of employment specifically requires it, or where it is necessary for the employee to be provided with work (for example, actors).[7] Mr Blackadder appealed the Full Court's decisions to the High Court.

The primary issue before the High Court was the proper construction of section 170CH(3)(a) of the WRA, which empowers the ARIC to make 'an order requiring the employer to reinstate the employee by ... reappointing the employee to the *position* in which the employee was employed immediately before the termination' (emphasis added).

The High Court unanimously found that an employer ordered to reinstate an employee must not only resume paying the employee's wages, but must also allow the employee to perform the duties which the employee was fulfilling prior to the termination.[8] The leading judgment was delivered by Justices Callinan and Heydon, who expressed the view that section 170CH should not be construed narrowly:

> Section 170CH should not be read in the narrow fashion adopted by the majority in the Full Court of the Federal Court. To do so is to treat the word 'position' as used in the [WRA] as a formal position only, a title, or something in the nature of an office, entitling the person reappointed to it, to its emoluments and nothing else. Nor does anything turn on the use of the word 'reappointing'. An employee carrying out work of the kind being carried out by the appellant before his dismissal would not in ordinary language be regarded as undertaking work pursuant to an appointment.[9]

Their Honours focused on the word 'reinstate', which they interpreted 'literally' to mean 'to put back in place' and further held that 'to pay the appellant but not to put him back in his usual situation in the workplace would not be to reinstate him.'[10] Similarly, their Honours also held that the words 'reappoint' and 'position' should also be given a broad meaning.[11] Their Honours also rejected reliance on other statutory regimes and the common law:

> The circumstances of this case are covered by the federal statutory regime established by the [WRA] and the Federal Court of Australia Act. Decisions in other jurisdictions under other statutory regimes are of little assistance. Nor are the decisions of other courts or this Court at common law. It is accordingly unnecessary to consider whether the categories of cases in which at common law actual work must be provided for an unlawfully terminated employee or contractor, are closed, although one might question the current relevance of judicial pronouncements made more than 60 years ago in the United Kingdom as to the extent to which an employer might be obliged to dine at home in order to provide work for his cook. It may be that in modern times, a desire for what has been called 'job satisfaction', and a need for employees of various kinds, to keep and to be seen to have kept their hands in by actual work have a role to play in determining whether work in fact should be provided. Nor is it necessary to have regard to the fact, which appears to have been overlooked by the Full Court, that the appellant's remuneration here could be affected by the actual work that he did, a matter which might of itself at common law justify an order that he be provided with actual work to do. The order for enforcement of the order of the [AIRC] for reinstatement should be understood in the way in which it has been explained in these reasons.[12]

In short, the High Court held that an order made by the AIRC for reinstatement requires an employer to restore an employee to the situation he or she was in immediately prior to termination. This means that the employee is entitled to actual work. While the High Court's judgment resolved the specific legal issues between Mr Blackadder and Ramsey, it has left open several other matters that are likely to confront practitioners: How long is an employer required to provide an employee with work following an order for reinstatement? Can an employee assume he or she has immunity from further dismissal? There is no doubt that these questions will be tested in years to come.

The Family Test Case

In June 2003, the Australia Council of Trade Unions (ACTU) and several unions made an application seeking variations to a number of major awards in relation to hours of work, parental leave, and flexibility in respect of other types of leave. While the process of conciliation was fruitful in resolving some of the claims, the remainder were the subject of a decision of the Full Bench of the AIRC handed down in August 2005.[13]

The main aspects of the ACTU's application consisted of the following claims:

- employees to have the right to seek variation to their days and hours of work so as to enable them to attend to their 'carers' responsibilities';

- emergency leave to be granted to employees to provide care for dependants or for other family members in the event of emergencies;
- employees to have the right to take up to 6 weeks' unpaid leave on 4 weeks' notice to attend to family responsibilities by electing to receive a lower rate of pay for a certain period, including the period of leave;
- increasing the period of unpaid parental leave from 12 months to 2 years;
- imposing obligations on employers to communicate with employees who are on parental leave in relation to significant change at the workplace, and to impose reciprocal obligations on employees on parental leave; and
- increasing the period of simultaneous maternity and paternity leave for employees to eight weeks.

The Full Bench classified the claims into two groups: the first dealing with parental leave, and the second dealing with arrangement of hours and days off work and other leave entitlements. In making its decision, the Full Bench acknowledged and weighed the tensions relevant to all parties in taking a 'positive step':

> The first conclusion is that we should take a positive step by way of award provision to assist employees to reconcile work and family responsibilities. We think it likely that most employers are sensitive to the family responsibilities of their employees and do their best to accommodate those needs by adopting a flexible approach to working hours, leave and other arrangements whenever they can. There are some employers, however, who are unlikely to accommodate the family responsibilities of their employees, even where it is practicable to do so. It is with those employers particularly in mind that we have concluded that the awards should contain provisions which provide employees with a better opportunity than they now have to obtain their employer's agreement to a change in working arrangements.

Having made this conclusion the Full Bench hastened to add that its decision was intentionally cautious:

> The second conclusion is that it is important that our decision should be a cautious one and that we should not attempt to deal with all of the situations in which employees may seek additional flexibility. It is evident that the range of different conditions of employment potentially affected by the applications before us is very broad. It would be complex and potentially unfair to employers to introduce changes covering such a broad range of conditions ...

The Full Bench did not grant the ACTU's claims, but it also did not reject them entirely. It took a similar approach in relation to the claims made by the employer parties. Ultimately, the Full Bench opted for an approach whereby it gave employers and employees a framework within which to negotiate mutually acceptable outcomes. This framework was put in terms of a right given to employees to request certain entitlements and a duty on employers not to unreasonably refuse the request. Specifically, award employees were given the right to request:

- simultaneous unpaid parental leave of up to eight weeks;
- an extended period of unpaid parental leave, from 52 weeks to 104 weeks; and
- return to work on a part-time basis, until the relevant child reaches school age.

Employers were required to consider the request having regard to the employee's circumstances and, provided the request is genuinely based on the employee's parental responsibilities, employers could only refuse the request on reasonable grounds related to the effect on the workplace or its business. Such grounds might include cost, lack of adequate replacement staff, loss of efficiency and the impact on customer service.

In making its decision, the AIRC sought to fairly balance the contesting claims between the ACTU and the employers:

> Neither the ACTU model, nor the model supported by the employers should be wholly accepted. The ACTU claim that these conditions should constitute an employee entitlement is not one we are prepared to grant. We agree with the employers that an unconditional right to additional parental leave benefits is inappropriate. It would have the potential to increase costs, reduce efficiency and create disharmony in the workplace. The employers' proposal, one which is based purely on agreement, has some merit. To take an example, an award might provide that an employer and an employee may agree that an employee could return from parental leave on a part-time basis until the child commences school. Such a provision might have some value in that it would recognise and encourage agreement about that matter. On the other hand it is equally true that there is nothing to stop the employer and the employee reaching such an agreement now. Despite that fact, and consistent with our earlier conclusion that some positive step is required, we think it is necessary to go beyond simply providing for agreement between the parties.

In addition, the AIRC decided that during periods of parental leave it is incumbent upon both employers and employees to continue to communicate about workplace changes and decision-making. The AIRC approved various other provisions that were agreed to by the parties during conciliation. The most significant of these was the agreement reached between the parties to allow casual employees unpaid emergency leave of up to 48 hours in the event:

- that the employee is unable to attend work or needs to leave work to care for members of his/her immediate family or household who are sick and require care or who require care due to an unexpected emergency or the birth of a child; or
- upon the death of an immediate family or household member.

Although the introduction of the WorkChoices reforms will effectively override the *Family Test Case*, a few aspects of it have been enshrined within those reforms, albeit in a different form. The underpinning rationale of those reforms, as with the Family Test Case, remain the same – ultimately work–life balance must be the outcome of workplace negotiation.

Liability of Managers under Safety Laws

One of the major areas on which the Howard Government's WorkChoices reforms will have little direct effect is occupational health and safety. By section 16(3)(c) of *Workplace Relations Act 2005 (Cth)*, State and Territory occupational health and safety laws are specifically not affected by the federal changes and will continue to operate. As such, decisions made under the State or Territory occupational health remain relevant for practitioners. A series of important decisions arising from the same set of events that relate to this area of the law have been handed down over the last couple of years. Practitioners and, particularly, managers should note them with interest. They clarify the extent to which managers, as opposed to companies, can be held liable for contributing to the risk of harm to the safety of workers.

Powercoal Pty Ltd owned and operated Awaba Colliery, an underground mine. Mr Peter Lamont Foster was the mine manager of Awaba Colliery. On 17 July 1998, one of the Colliery's roofs collapsed and a miner, Mr Barry John Edwards, suffered fatal injuries as a result.

Two charges were brought against the company and Mr Foster under section 15(1) and section 50(1) of the *Occupational Health & Safety Act* 1983 (NSW). Section 15(1) states that 'every employer shall ensure the health, safety and welfare at work of all the employer's employees'. Section 50(1) of the Act provides:

> Where a corporation contravenes, whether by act or omission, any provision of this Act or the regulations, and each person concerned in the management of the corporation, shall be deemed to have contravened the same provision.

The charges alleged that the company had failed to implement an adequate system for assessing the safety of the roof in the area of the collapse, and had failed to implement an adequate system for notifying employees of roof problems and roof history throughout the various phases of mining in that area.

At first instance, Justice Peterson acquitted the company and the mine manager of all charges.[14] The decision was appealed to the Full Bench of the New South Wales Industrial Relations Commission (NSWIRC), which allowed the appeal and convicted both the company and the mine manager of the charges.[15] The Full Bench, with reference to regulation 37 of the *Coalmines Regulation Act* 1982, found that Mr Foster, the mine manager, had the 'highest level of supervisory control of all matters at the Awaba Colliery and that he had ultimate supervisory control over all occupational health and safety matters at that colliery'.[16] This included 'full charge and control of all employees at the mine'.[17] The Full Bench deemed him guilty of the same charges as the company, under section 50 of the Act, and determined that he had not made out a defence for the same reasons the company had not.

The Company and Mr Foster then sought orders from the New South Wales Court of Appeal to exercise its supervisory jurisdiction over the NSWIRC to quash the convictions made by the Full Bench of the NSWIRC.[18] The company and Mr Foster argued several grounds in attempting to have the

NSWIRC's decision overturned, including challenging the constitutionality of the NSWIRC exercising criminal jurisdiction.[19] The claimants also challenged the decision on the ground that there were jurisdictional errors.[20] A detailed examination of these issues goes beyond the scope of this article but it is sufficient to note that both arguments were rejected.

Of immediate relevance was the argument advanced on behalf of Mr Foster specifically. He submitted that the decision of the Full Bench of NSWIRC should be quashed because it incorrectly construed section 50(1) of the OHS Act. According to Mr Foster, a proper construction of the section would have resulted in him not being covered by that section and therefore not liable.[21] Along with the other submissions, the Court of Appeal rejected this argument.

The mine manager presented two subsidiary arguments in support of his main submission that the scope of section 50 should not be extended to include the manager of a mine:

(1) reference in section 50(1) of the Act to persons 'concerned in the management of the corporation' extended only to those at the highest levels of the corporation who were involved in the overall management of the corporation, not to someone like himself who was merely the manager of a colliery;[22]

(2) the phrase 'management of the company' found in section 592 of the *Corporation Act* 2001 (Cth) and its predecessors has been interpreted by case law to mean those persons concerned with the central management of the corporation.[23]

In support of his first subsidiary argument, the claimant relied on the line of case law which defines the management of a corporation as those that 'direct the mind and the will' of the corporation.[24] However, the Court of Appeal determined that line of case law, concerned with the determination of when a particular person can be said to be the corporation for such purposes as knowledge or notice, was of no relevance to the statutory construction of the occupational health and safety provision before the Court of Appeal.[25]

In relation to the second argument, the Court acknowledged that there is a line of authority which has found the phrase 'management of the company' in section 592 of the *Corporations Act* 2001 (Cth) to be concerned with central management of the company, rather than persons who managed specific assets of the company.[26] However, the Court of Appeal stated that the term 'management of the company' must be understood by the context of the provisions in which it is contained.[27] The Court of Appeal summarized the context of section 592 of the *Corporations Act* to be concerned with the determination of persons who participated in management at a time when a debt was incurred, and when there were reasonable grounds to suspect that the company would not be able to pay its debts.[28] In comparison, the Court of Appeal reasoned that where the concern is with occupational health and safety issues, the legislation is concerned with any aspect of the operations of the company insofar as it raises safety considerations. The Court of Appeal determined that the manager of a mine is clearly within the scope of that purpose.[29]

In coming to its final conclusion, the Court of Appeal briefly reviewed the objects of the OHS Act contained in section 5(1), and noted that the language in section 18(1) made the duties imposed by the Act general in nature. As such, these duties are not restricted to a direct employer, with the Court of Appeal concluding that these provisions 'suggest that Parliament did not intend to give the language of section 50(1) a narrow, let alone a technical meaning'. The Court of Appeal held that the words 'management of the corporation' should not be restricted to apply only to central management' and that the Full Bench had not committed an error of law in its reasoning.[30] The mine manager had ultimate supervisory control over all health and safety concerns at the mine site, as well as full charge and authority over all employees. In this case, the mine manager would have been directly involved in decisions regarding safety issues, and was therefore clearly complicit in any liability assessed against the corporation.

As occupational health and safety laws remain operative in the wake of WorkChoices, the Court of Appeal's decision is relevant. Although discussing important constitutional and administrative law principles, the focus of discussion here has been on the Court of Appeal's interpretation of the extent to which managers will be liable for their company's safety breaches. By giving the relevant section a wide, purposive construction, the Court of Appeal has expanded the ambit of the section and, therefore, the type of managers that can be caught by it. This heightens the need for companies and individual managers to rigorously enforce safety at their workplaces, an important and widely accepted policy objective.

Workplace Bullying

Bullying in the workplace has become a hot topic in recent years. Despite this, the current state of the law in NSW allows only limited recourse to compensation for victims of workplace bullying. While OHS legislation provides for the prosecution of a company and its directors when they fail to uphold the safety, health and welfare at work of their employees, such actions cannot be brought by a victim nor can they allow for the provision of compensation to victims.[31] Attempts to rely on anti-discrimination laws also have fallbacks as many instances of bullying are not based on the 'prohibited reasons' enumerated in anti-discrimination legislation. Seen in this light, the decision of Justice Adams of the Supreme Court of New South Wales in *Naidu v Group 4 Securitas Pty Ltd & Anor*,[32] is a significant step forward. Not only did it provide common law damages to a victim of workplace bullying, it is also an important development of the common law.

Mr Naidu was employed as a security officer with Group 4 Securitas from March 1990 until February 1998. Group 4 was contracted by Nationwide News to provide security services at News' Surry Hills site. Though employed by Group 4, News organized Mr Naidu's duties. As such, it was unnecessary for him to attend Group 4's premises and he reported directly to News. In April 1992, Mr Naidu became the Assistant Security and Fire Control Manager at

News to Mr Chaloner. It was alleged that over the course of many years Mr Chaloner subjected Mr Naidu to 'brutal, demeaning abuse'. This included racist and sexual vilification on a daily basis, indecent exposure and sexual assault, physical intimidation, financial threats (including repeated threats to Mr Naidu's employment) and threats that he would never have a job if he left News. It was also alleged that Mr Naidu did an extreme amount of unpaid hours and unpaid labour work on the construction of Mr Chaloner's personal residence. As a result of these, Mr Naidu claimed he suffered major psychological injury including major depression and post traumatic stress disorder.

Justice Adams found both Group 4 and News jointly liable for Mr Naidu's injury. Although Justice Adams found that neither Group 4 nor News could be liable for conduct that was 'external' to the workplace, His Honour found that Mr Chaloner's abusive behaviour within the work context was deemed to be sufficient in itself to cause Mr Naidu's psychological injury.[33] His Honour held that the workplace connected abuse was the substantial cause of Mr Naidu's illness, whatever additional contribution was made by the other misconduct.[34]

In relation to Mr Naidu's employer, Group 4, Justice Adams held that it had a non-delegable duty to provide a safe working environment, a duty that is implied into all contracts of employment.[35] Although this finding is not novel, Justice Adams proceeded to state that this duty extended to protecting employees from racial or personal vilification[36] and to protecting employees from fear of insult or physical harm.[37] Furthermore, this duty was incorporated into Mr Naidu's contract of employment by the existence of a Group 4 policy that explicitly prohibited personal vilification.

In its defence, Group 4 contended that Mr Naidu had never complained to it, and that it was not aware of Mr Chaloner's conduct. However, Justice Adams held that Group 4 had direct or constructive knowledge of the behaviour on two grounds. First, Justice Adams held that other Group 4 security officers who worked at the News premises were aware of Mr Chaloner's conduct toward Mr Naidu, and their knowledge was imputed upon Group 4.[38] His Honour held that any failure of the other employees to report Mr Chaloner's conduct was as a result of Group 4's failure to adequately train its employees or to otherwise emphasize the importance of its harassment and discrimination policy. Secondly, Justice Adams found that Mr Chaloner was an agent of both News and Group 4, and as Group 4's agent his own knowledge of his misconduct was also attributed to Group 4.[39]

In relation to News' liability, Justice Adams held that it was vicariously liable for Mr Chaloner's misconduct. His Honour held that, in the main, Mr Chaloner's threats, demeaning behaviour and racial vilification were intimately connected with his day-to-day direction and control of Mr Naidu. Even though this conduct was not authorized, and in fact prohibited, News was vicariously liable for it.[40]

Justice Adams awarded damages to Mr Naidu for his out-of-pocket expenses (including medical expenses), his future medical expenses calculated over his life expectancy, his economic loss due to his incapacity to perform any form of paid employment for the foreseeable future[41] and general damages to compensate Mr Naidu for the diminution in his enjoyment of life. His Honour permitted the parties with an opportunity to agree to appropriate sums. However, his Honour did order News to pay Mr Naidu a sum of $150,000 in exemplary damagers – to deter repetition of the wrongdoing.

As an issue dealing with the commission of torts at the workplace and therefore decided at common law, the law pronounced in this case will not be affected by WorkChoices. An important case, the decision in *Naidu* confirms the ability of a plaintiff to recover damages for psychological injury resulting from workplace bullying independent of occupational health and safety and anti-discrimination legislation. By recognising that tort law covers psychological injury occasioned at work, employers should be particularly aware of the need to ameliorate the scourge of workplace bullying.

Conclusion

This article has pointed out a number of important developments in Australian labour law over the course of 2005. Although 2005 will be remembered as the year of WorkChoices, the decisions noted here carry important implications for practitioners. Relatively untouched by the Howard Government's industrial relations reforms, the areas of law with which the cases deal have been clarified in significant ways. First, as a matter of statutory construction, the High Court has outlined that employers must effectively provide work for reinstated employees. The AIRC has expanded the ability of employees to ask for various forms of leave connected with family life. The New South Wales Court of Appeal has adopted a broad approach with respect to the levels of management that can be held liable for occupational health and safety breaches and the New South Wales Supreme Court has held that relief is available for psychological injury as a result of workplace bullying. In all of these cases, therefore, there has been a legal and practical expansion of the relief and entitlements available for employees. Such cases put practitioners on notice to not simply focus on WorkChoices and remain aware of all labour law developments.

Notes

1 Note that the ability to gain relief for harsh, unjust or unreasonable dismissal has been tempered by section 643(10) of the *Workplace Relations Act 2005 (Cth)*, which excludes employees from gaining relief if they employed by an employer that employs fewer than 100 employees.

2 (2005) 215 ALR 87, [2005] HCA 22.

3 *Blackadder v Ramsey Butchering Services Pty Ltd*, 29 March 2000 (Redmond C), Prints S4537 and S4542.

4 *Blackadder v Ramsey Butchering Services Pty Ltd*, 26 June 2000 (Boulton and Munro JJ, Harrison C), Print S7395.

5 *Blackadder v Ramsey Butchering Services Pty Ltd* (2002) 118 FCR 395.

6 *Ramsey Butchering Services Pty Ltd v Blackadder* (2003) 127 FCR 381 (Tamberlin and Goldberg JJ, Moore J dissenting).

7 Ibid at 416 [77]-[78].

8 *Blackadder v Ramsey Butchering Services Pty Ltd* (2005) 215 ALR 87, [2005] HCA 22.

9 Ibid, at 106, para [74].

10 Ibid, at 106–107, para [75].

11 Ibid.

12 Ibid, at 108, para. [80].

13 *Family Provisions Test Case*, 8 August 2005 (Giudice P, Ross VP, Cartwright SDP, Ives DP and Cribb C), Print 082005. Note that the extracted quotations in this section can be found at the paragraph number of the decision indicated at the beginning of each quotation.

14 *Morrison v Powercoal Pty Ltd* [2003] NSWIRComm 342.

15 *Morrision v Powercoal Pty Ltd & Anor* [2004] NSWIRComm 297, per Vice-President Justice Walton, Justice Boland and Justice Staff.

16 Ibid at para. [173].

17 Ibid at para [174].

18 *Powercoal Pty Ltd & Peter Lamont Foster v Industrial Relations Commission of NSW & Rodney Dale Morrison* [2005] NSWCA 345 per Chief Justice Spigelman (with whom President Mason and Appeal Justice Handley agreed).

19 Ibid at para [38].

20 Ibid at para [49].

21 Ibid at para [88].

22 Ibid at para [90].

23 Ibid at para [97].

24 For example, *Tesco Supermarkets Limited v Nattrass* [1972] AC 153.

25 *Powercoal Pty Ltd & Peter Lamont Foster v Industrial Relations Commission of NSW & Rodney Dale Morrison* [2005] NSWCA 345 at para 95.

26 Ibid at para [97]. For example, *Omnicon Video Pty Ltd v Kookaburra Production Pty Ltd* (1995) 13 ACLC 1795 and *Holpitt Pty Ltd v Swaab* (1992) 33 FCR 474.

27 *Powercoal Pty Ltd & Peter Lamont Foster v Industrial Relations Commission of NSW & Rodney Dale Morrison* [2005] NSWCA 345 at para [98].

28 Ibid at para [99].

29 Ibid at para [102].

30 Ibid at para [116].

31 *WorkCover Authority (NSW) (InspectorMaddaford) v Coleman* [2004] NSWIRComm 317.

32 [2005] NSWSC 618.

33 Ibid paras [19] and [20].

34 Ibid at para [214].

35 Ibid at para [188].

36 Ibid at para [191].

37 Ibid at para [200].

38 Ibid at para [197].

39 Ibid at para [198].

40 Ibid at para [214].

41 Ibid at para [282].

6

Trade Unionism in 2005

Alison Barnes
University of Western Sydney, Australia

Introduction

When assuming leadership of the Liberal Party in 1985, John Howard commented,

> I think the biggest single economic challenge over the next five to ten years is to free up the labour market and in doing so alter the balance in our industrial relations system. (quoted in Dabscheck, 1993: 5)

Two decades later, in a telling slip, Howard said, 'We're not governing for the unions, we're governing for the employers', indicating inadvertently in whose favour the balance was being tipped (Howard, 2005). Unlike 1996, which saw him undertake a pre-election tactical retreat from New Right policies of wholesale elimination of awards and their legislative prop, the Australian Industrial Relations Commission, in 2005 there was no going backwards. The year witnessed the final dismantling of Australia's century-old model of industrial relations and the institutionalization of the federal government's deeply anti-union agenda.

The impending federal industrial relations legislation – and the unions' strategic response – dominated 2005. Led primarily by the Australian Council of Trade Unions (ACTU) and supportive Trades and Labour Councils, the unions' community-oriented media campaign emphasized issues that people could easily relate to such as weekend and overtime penalty rates and unfair dismissal. The aggressively anti-union content of the 'reforms' was never an explicit focus of the campaign. It successfully united such disparate groups as churches, civil libertarians, welfare groups, and academics to raise public awareness of the legislation and tap into community concerns about job security and work/family balance. The union movement made the running, and State Labor governments were supportive, although federal Labor dragged its heels until convinced of the widespread unpopularity of the Government's proposals.

Maintaining the momentum already generated by the campaign will be challenge enough. More difficult will be producing lasting outcomes in terms of membership growth and the development of stronger pro-union sentiment within the community. It is unclear how unions will respond to the new environment once the legislation takes effect. Will an approach that eschews traditional industrial militancy continue to be effective, or will more confrontational tactics be adopted? Already there have been suggestions of unions divesting themselves of their assets, and of individual members declining to pay fines and opting for gaol, but the failure to announce plans for large-scale mobilizations in 2006 has concerned some union activists.

The primary aim of this article is to analyse the reaction of unions to WorkChoices. A secondary purpose is to consider how unions will respond to the numerous challenges that will confront them when the legislation begins to bite, while simultaneously seeking to win over the hearts and minds of the broader community.

Membership: John Howard, the Union Movement's 'Latest Star Recruiter'

The ABS figures from August 2004, released in March 2005, were disappointing for the union movement, with the Australian Bureau of Statistics reporting 1,842,100 union members in 2004 as compared to 1,866,700 in 2003, indicating a one percent decline (ABS, 2005). The year ended on a higher note, however, with a November 2005 Roy Morgan Poll finding that almost 2.5 million employed workers identified as union members and a further 1.5 million wished to be members (Roy Morgan Research, 2005). As in previous years, the ability to realize this potential poses a significant challenge for unions.

Overall sentiment in favour of unions also increased, with only 14 percent of those polled for the *State of the Union Report* 2005 believing Australia would be better off without unions, as compared with 25 percent in 1996. Moreover, in 2005 fewer people (25 percent) were dissatisfied with unions than a decade earlier (43 percent). The Report also indicated that 50 percent of workers would prefer to be in a union. Anecdotal evidence from individual unions (the Liquor, Hospitality and Miscellaneous Union (LHMU) in South Australia, nurses' unions in Victoria and NSW, the National Union of Workers (NUW) in Victoria, and the Electrical Trades Union, the Queensland Public Sector Union and the Australian Services Union in Queensland) suggested a rise in union membership in the second half of 2005, possibly in response to the Your Rights at Work Campaign and/or concern about the Government's WorkChoices legislation (ABC Online, 2005b; Dyer, 2005; O'Malley, 2005a; Workers Online, 2005d). Danielle O'Brien, Membership Supervisor of the NSW branch of the NUW, remarked that 'John Howard is the NUW's latest star recruiter because the NSW branch has ... recorded a significant increase in recent months' (Workers Online, 2005d).

It remains to be seen whether real growth in membership will occur in 2006 and beyond. It could well be that, when confronted with WorkChoices' numerous impediments, unions will be hard pressed to retain members let alone recruit new ones.

WorkChoices

WorkChoices is deeply anti-union and represents a qualitative shift in the balance of power in favour of employers. By limiting employees' capacity to strike and simultaneously freeing up employers' ability to lock workers out, WorkChoices 'is quite unashamedly aimed at further reducing union bargaining power' (Gittens, 2005).

A detailed analysis of the legislation is undertaken elsewhere in this edition, but a brief overview here of some key aspects is pertinent because of their potential to severely diminish the ability of unions both to organize workers and to deliver improved conditions via collective bargaining.

The unions' publicity campaign in the lead-up to the introduction of the legislation deliberately focused on those aspects of the WorkChoices Bill that would directly affect individual workers, such as the implications of Australian Workplace Agreements (AWAs) and the removal of remedies for unfair dismissal. Yet the most significant changes in the legislation – and potentially the most damaging for unions – are the restrictions on the right to take industrial action and on the rights of unions to carry out their traditional functions, the right of entry for union officials, and the right to participate in agreement making. While the Government's advertising campaign claimed that the right to join a union was 'protected by law', ACTU President Sharan Burrow likened it to being allowed to join a golf club, but not being able to play on the course (Burrow, 2005).

Constraints on Industrial Action

Under WorkChoices, the onerous, drawn-out process required of unions prior to taking industrial action all but removes the legal right to take action. The Minister for Workplace Relations, moreover, has the discretion to remove this right entirely. The legislation abandons all pretence of being even handed: it retains the broad definition of industrial action as it has applied to employees but, in the case of employers, limits the definition to lockouts and excludes other actions, such as threatened dismissal, against which unions have previously been able to utilize section 127 of the *Workplace Relations Act* to seek orders against employers. It makes Australia the only nation in the OECD to legally discriminate in favour of lockouts and against strikes (Briggs, 2005).

The previous requirement to give three days notice during a bargaining period of intention to take industrial action has been replaced with an obligation on unions to first make application to the AIRC for a ballot, and then to have the AIRC approve an agent to conduct it, usually as a postal ballot. If the application is approved, to be successful the ballot requires a majority of members to vote – a formidable task especially in large workplaces with hundreds or thousands of members. If the ballot approves industrial action, the Commission may then require up to seven days notice be given to the employer. The 28-page-long division of the Act dealing with protected action consists almost entirely of obstacles to be overcome, listing different scenarios in which industrial action is not protected. Even aside from the new secret ballot process, it is difficult to think of any past example of employee industrial action – Australian or international – that would not have offended these requirements in some way.

The rules prohibiting payment to employees when engaged in industrial action have been tightened, with the minimum deduction now being four hours. This may mean the end of the one-hour stop-work meeting, especially in light of the arduous nature of the secret ballot provisions that must be observed before such a meeting can be called. Even after the union has jumped through the required regulatory hoops, the Minister can still issue a declaration to end the bargaining period if he/she considers that certain circumstances exist, including, remarkably, if the industrial action adversely affects the employer (s.112(1)(b)).

Undoubtedly, unions will have to find ways to circumvent the provisions by adopting alternative campaigning strategies that do not involve conventionally-directed industrial action, such as placing greater emphasis on media and publicity and on involving the community. Of equal significance will be whether unions choose to resist the legislation by way of unprotected or unlawful industrial action. What is unclear at this stage is the extent to which the Government's industrial program will lead to civil and industrial disobedience, or longer periods of industrial action on those occasions when unions and their members manage to satisfy all of the Act's requirements.

Right of Entry

The amendments to the right of entry provisions not only place restrictions on union officials but also remove protections for union activists and for employees who wish to contact the union. They thus strike at the heart of shopfloor activism. Employers can now insist that visits occur only during breaks or non-working time and also designate where the meeting is to take place – provisions that will doubtless intimidate some employees while allowing easy identification of activists. The targeting of union members is further facilitated by their being the only workers entitled to call in union officials to investigate breaches of industrial instruments.

There is no right of entry to workplaces to speak to employees covered by AWAs, even where the union, as the workers' appointed bargaining agent, may have negotiated the terms of the AWA. There is a right of entry only for discussions with employees where an award or union agreement applies. Officials can inspect members' records only to investigate suspected breaches, and these members would have to be identified to the employer. To obtain a right-of-entry permit an official must pass a 'fit and proper person' test, and a new regime of fines and suspensions has been introduced for transgressions.

As well as hindering a union's capacity to organize workers, the restrictions on entry and inspection rights will inhibit its ability to enforce employee rights and entitlements, leaving workers increasingly vulnerable to exploitation. The exclusion of union officials from the site could well result in a greater emphasis on unions employing alternative methods to contact workers – a shift that will prove a greater challenge to some unions than others. The home-visiting blitzes with which a number of unions have experimented since the tactic was success-fully employed to establish the Pilbara Mineworkers Union (Ellem, 2003) may become more than simply an innovative means to contact new members and activists. It is, however, a resource-intensive option.

'Softening up' of Targeted Industries

Higher Education

In its determination to remake the workplace, ideological as well as pragmatic considerations doubtless persuaded the Government to make early targets of both tertiary education and building unions. A pool of $260 million funding to universities was subject to their satisfying the 'Higher Education Workplace Relations Requirements' (HEWRRs). To be eligible to access the addition-al funding, universities had to offer AWAs to staff and take steps that would diminish the presence of unions on campuses. Months before the WorkChoices Bill introduced the prospect of 'prohibited matters' in workplace agreements, the April 2005 announcement of the HEWRRs presaged restrictions on the content of Enterprise Agreements and university policies. HEWRRs prohib-ited provisions placing limits on levels of fixed-term or casual employment, on union nominees being the sole representatives of staff on committees, and any provisions deemed 'overly prescriptive'.

With the tertiary education sector having experienced real cuts in funding since the Howard Government's election in 1996, the position of university staff unions was difficult. The National Tertiary Education Union (NTEU) sought to negotiate and settle HEWRRs-compliant enterprise agreements by the 30 November 2005 deadline for those universities that did not have current certified agreements in place when the HEWRRs were announced. Agreements were successfully concluded with all but the University of Ballarat where Vice Chancellor Kerry Cox twice put a non-union s170LK agreement to ballot, which staff twice rejected, leaving the regional Victorian institution without access to the funding.[1] Citing the HEWRRs, almost all university adminis-trations wrote to campus unions advising them that they would no longer be provided with office space. Management at the University of New England and the University of Newcastle at one stage locked both the NTEU and the Community and Public Sector Union out of their campus offices overnight.

Vocational education institutions such as state-based TAFEs have been targeted in a similar manner. As a possible precursor to future attacks on teachers' unions, Commonwealth government funding of TAFEs has been made contingent upon State governments offering AWAs to TAFE employees.

Building Industries

The year saw the continuation of the federal Government's pursuit of the Construction, Forestry, Mining and Energy Union (CFMEU) and its members. In October, following the passage of the *Building & Construction Industry Improvement Act*, the Building Industry Taskforce was recast as the Australian Building and Construction Commission and given increased powers and a budget of over $100 million. Building workers, employers and union officials can now be gaoled for up to six months for refusing to produce documents demanded by the Commission or to answer questions, the right to silence having been removed. Almost all industrial action and union meetings will be illegal, with violations carrying fines of up to $22,000 for individuals and $110,000 for unions (Hard Hat, 2005b). The Act in conjunction with the proposed Independent Contractors Act will bring to an end the practice of subjecting all sub-contractors to site conditions negotiated in the enterprise agreement with the head contractors. A likely outcome will be the weakening of the capacity of unions to maintain conditions and preserve union coverage. In an attempt to coerce the States into conforming to its agenda, the federal Government has threatened to make funding for roads and water projects dependent upon the States' compliance with its building reforms (Briggs et al., 2005).

As with the higher education sector, some building industry unions such as those in Victoria attempted to soften the immediate impact of WorkChoices by securing certified agreements with employers before the Act came into effect.

The Campaign Against WorkChoices

The lead-up to the passage of the WorkChoices legislation provided unions with opportunities that they both recognized and capitalized on. Their short-term if unattainable aim was to prevent the passage of the Bill, but in the long term they sought to build opposition to the changes.

Despite being a defining year for unionism, 2005 did not witness any large-scale general strikes or other widespread forms of overt or conventional militancy. What the union movement did was to fight in ways that sought to engage the broader community and win its support. Confronted by the industrial brutality of WorkChoices, unions seized the opportunity to implement 'some of the things that we have been talking about for the last 10 years ... Things like running ads, actions on the ground, the Last Weekend, the Sky Channel broadcast, the targeted seats campaign' (John Robertson quoted in Gallaway, 2005). The highly successful public relations campaign may not have persuaded the Government-dominated Senate, but it succeeded in galvanizing workers and rousing community interest.

There are a number of possible explanations for the unions choosing to fight this most important of battles in this way. First, perhaps, was a reluctance to alienate Howard's 'battlers'. As ACTU Secretary Greg Combet remarked, 'We have to bring the people with us' (O'Malley and Metherell, 2005) – a significant consideration if one has an eye to the next election. Second, the tactical shift may have been influenced by the lessons learnt during the waterfront dispute, when the benefits of professional media management, of polling, and public relations were used and appreciated. Third, memories were still fresh of the 1996 'Cavalcade to Canberra' against the Workplace Relations Act where the 'fallout from the riot was long, painful and damaging for unions' (Pocock and Wright, 1997). Whatever the reasons, the preparedness of unions – including those that traditionally might have been expected to adopt a more confrontational approach – to unite behind the campaign was noteworthy.[2]

ACTU-commissioned research indicated that the general community lacked awareness of the reforms but opposed them once they learned of their content. When launching the largest and most expensive media campaign in the ACTU's 77-year history (Workplace Express, 2005a), Sharan Burrow remarked, 'the challenge for unions is to make the public aware about what is at stake and hold the government accountable for this attack on working families' (ACTU, 2005b). The television advertisements that started screening on 19 June were designed to feed into the 'week of action' that concluded on 1 July. Produced by Essential Media Communications, the advertisements focused on domestic concerns and highlighted issues such as job security, with the legislation's unfairness being a consistent theme.

Sharan Burrow believed that

> what worked for us in a communication sense was kicking off the campaign with the advertising because it brought the stories of real people into the living rooms of Australia and touched a chord with everyone's experience. Everybody has a family member – if not themselves, then a friend or work colleague – who has experienced some sort of maltreatment in the workplace. People generally understand vulnerability. (personal interview, 2005)

Calls to the ACTU seeking information and assistance rose after the TV ads aired (Dyer, 2005). The *Sydney Morning Herald* noted that the campaign 'has been credited with causing a record 10-point slump in Mr Howard's personal approval record' (Metherell, 2005b). An Auspoll survey of people living in marginal seats in New South Wales also indicated a decline in support for the Coalition and that, of the 72 percent who had seen the ads, half viewed the reforms more negatively (Hildebrand, 2005b).

The ACTU-coordinated campaign not only caught the Government unprepared, it also set the terms for the public debate about the legislation. Prime Minister Howard and Workplace Relations Minister Kevin Andrews condemned the ACTU for its 'misleading scare campaign' (Workplace Express, 2005a). Unions NSW Secretary John Robertson agreed: 'Well, they're right. These changes are bloody scary and the public has a right to know the truth' (Workplace Express, 2005b). Despite a $55 million advertising campaign of its own, the Government remained on the back foot. But, as Michael Crosby observed, the test of the unions' success will be

> not whether the Prime Minister's approval rating falls or whether public opinion is wholly on our side – no matter how gratifying that outcome may be. The test is much tougher. Can we maintain current density and actually grow in spite of the hand that has been dealt us? (Crosby, 2005)

The Rallies

A national week of action culminated in large rallies across the country. On 1 July in Sydney, 20,000 people retraced the Hungry Mile to the Harbour Bridge from which a giant 'Your Rights at Work' banner was unveiled. The day before, 120,000 marchers had brought gridlock to central Melbourne (Marr, 2005). Despite Commonwealth public servants receiving emails and memos advising them that those who attended the rallies would be breaking the law, the Department of Employment and Workplace Relations instructing agencies that requests for leave to attend the rallies should be denied (O'Malley, 2005b), and Visy, Amcor and others successfully applying for s.127 orders to prohibit attendance, the National Day of Community Protest on 15 November was, in absolute numbers, the Australian labour movement's largest-ever demonstration. Between 500,000 and 600,000 people protested at 300 venues, ranging from 150 at the Northern Territory uranium-mining town of Bachelor, to 150,000–210,000 in Melbourne (O'Malley and Murphy, 2005). Utilizing the model adopted by Unions NSW in earlier state-wide meetings, the venues were linked by satellite and giant TV screens, with prerecorded sections of the broadcast featuring workers explaining how the changes would affect them.

Reaching Out to Regional Communities and Families

Unions began to campaign in regional areas, making use of those staples of community activism: leaflets, sausage sizzles, and meetings. Unions NSW organized a road trip: a custom-painted orange bus emblazoned with the 'Your Rights at Work' logo travelled around New South Wales to inform and establish links with country centres and rural communities. Arising from the tour, more than 40 local campaign committees were established (Lewis, 2005). In Victoria, the Trades Hall 'Country Cavalcade' travelled throughout regional Victoria, discussing the federal government's reforms with workers and attracting the interest of local media. The aim in both cases was to further develop and stimulate local contact among unions and unionists in their communities, which in NSW built on the 27 May and 1 July state-wide Sky Channel meetings. Some new regional Labour Councils sprang up, while others were reactivated, creating the local organization required, among other things, to initiate community campaigns in targeted electorates.

The last half of the year was peppered with varying activities aimed at highlighting the threat posed by the federal legislation. On the Sunday before the newly constituted government-controlled Senate began sitting, Unions NSW convened the 'Last Weekend' family picnic day to mark the last occasion on which workers would be able to spend time with their families before, as a poster put it, 'John Howard takes it away'. The State Labor Government's contribution was to give the picnic special event status and provide additional public transport (Workers Online, 2005a). In Victoria, union members distributed football-shaped brochures to the 300,000 fans attending the AFL's 'family round' of matches to highlight the impact of the reforms on families (ACTU, 2005c). At the 'Union Family Race Day', SA Unions distributed postcards urging politicians to vote against the changes (ABC Online, 2005a). There were also numerous individual union initiatives such as the Rail Tram and Bus Union organizing a ride from Sydney to Canberra in which more than 500 cyclists participated.

Industry-specific campaigns were also important for keeping issues in the media. One group with a lot at stake were independent lorry owner-drivers whose rates and other conditions could be regulated under chapter 6 of the NSW *Industrial Relations Act 1996* but were now threatened by both WorkChoices and the Commonwealth's proposed Independent Contractors' Act. In August a 600-strong convoy of owner-drivers converged on Canberra. A month earlier, members of the Transport Workers Union had staged a slow drive across the Sydney Harbour Bridge.

Highlighting Relevant Disputes

Unions highlighted current disputes in several States to illustrate the failings of the workplace legislation as it then stood and to emphasize how the WorkChoices Bill would undermine pay and conditions and further tip the balance in favour of employers. The Boeing dispute in Williamtown, NSW is perhaps the best known example. It centred on Boeing employees on AWAs who were paid $20,000 less than other workers in the industry performing similar work but covered by an enterprise agreement. Unions focused media attention on the pay disparity, on Boeing's opposition to its employees bargaining collectively, and the difficulty they encountered in forcing Boeing to the negotiating table.[3] To highlight the existing inadequacies of the *Workplace Relations Act* 1996 and the even more draconian provisions of the WorkChoices Bill, marchers from the November 15 rally at Sydney's Belmore Park linked up with those in Martin Place to converge on Boeing's headquarters.

In Victoria, the focus was on a Federal Court challenge by six Mildura women to their sacking by Merbein Mushroom Investments for refusing to sign an AWA that would cut their pay by up to 25 percent when piece rates replaced an hourly rate. As Australian Workers Union National Secretary Bill Shorten commented,

> nearly all the sacked women have children to support. They are hard-working mothers in a difficult industry with serious occupational health and safety issues. Their only

'crime' was to refuse to sign an individual contract. Everyone else who signed the contract kept their jobs, but have suffered significant pay cuts. (ACTU, 2005a)

Even Minister Kevin Andrews' own Department of Employment and Workplace Relations was not immune from anti-AWA activity. Its public service employees overwhelmingly rejected a non-union agreement and in August gained a 16 percent pay rise and continued access to the Industrial Relations Commission (Hard Hat, 2005a; Workers Online, 2005b). Other disputes to attract attention, such as those involving Bakers Delight in South Australia and Krispy Kreme Donuts in Sydney, provided case studies of what was in store for young and vulnerable workers under the WorkChoices regime.[4] Masterton Homes fired a carpenter employed by the company for 26 years when he refused to sign an AWA. A union-led campaign and picket line resulted in his reinstatement (Hard Hat, 2005a). The LHMU conducted an email campaign against 'Pink Salt' (a contestant in the 'My Restaurant Rules' TV program) that 'resulted in more than 1200 emails to the restaurant, and 135,000 appearances of an LHMU-sponsored ad on Google telling Australians about the on-camera blow-up over poor pay under AWAs' (LHMU, 2005).

At the forefront of several notable wins for the union movement was the apparent final resolution in December of the James Hardie asbestos compensation dispute.[5] Another was the Federal Court's fining the Commonwealth Bank $750,000 for the activities of its subsidiary CommSec in forcing the resignation and subsequent re-employment on individual contracts of 259 employees. The case was a significant victory for the Finance Sector Union, which represented the workers but, as the union's lawyer noted, such cases will be more difficult to run in future: 'The Government has changed the provision of the Act that we've relied on in this case to make it much harder for unions ...WorkChoices itself takes away so many rights from workers that companies will be able to do it much simpler than the Commonwealth Bank did in this case' (Workplace Express, 2005e).

The Last Test Case?

A significant aspect of the AIRC's role until now has been its determination of union-mounted Awards test cases the results of which have traditionally flowed on to the wider workforce. Such cases underpinned some unions' industry-based organizing and provided a focus for much of their activity. WorkChoices will preclude this method of securing workplace advances.

In what was potentially its last test case, the full bench of the AIRC in August delivered its decision in the ACTU's 'Work and Family Test Case'. The ACTU sought to use the case, which began in 2003, 'to help workers accommodate their family responsibilities' by regulating flexible work practices to ensure that they actually worked for families. After conciliation, the parties agreed to double carers leave from five to ten days (Workplace Express, 2005c).

As a result of the decision, which at face value has the potential to affect 1.6 million workers on awards, primary carers will be able to request 24 months' unpaid parental leave (a doubling of the present entitlement) and also part-time employment until the child reaches school age (Workplace Express, 2005e). Non-primary carers (usually fathers) will be able to seek eight weeks' unpaid leave after the birth of a child (as opposed to the current one week). Employers, however, will be able to refuse all three requests if they have reasonable grounds for doing so. What constitutes 'reasonable grounds' is yet to be tested, but could include 'cost, lack of adequate replacement staff, loss of efficiency and effect on customer service' (ACTU, 2005d).

Although the AIRC rejected many of the ACTU claims, Sharan Burrow commented that 'Unions are pleased that the Australian Industrial Relations Commission has today approved the key elements of the ACTU's long-running Work and Family Test Case' (ACTU, 2005d). The utility of this decision, however, may be highly constrained because WorkChoices will exclude many workers whose awards have not already been varied to include the new provisions, which are not included in the Fair Pay and Conditions Standard. Whether they will be widely acknowledged and adhered to in the future will depend on community awareness of them and individual bargaining strength at the workplace. As with many conditions, there is no guarantee they will be observed, so these gains could well be eroded in future.

What's Next

While most union attention was focused on the immediate threat posed by WorkChoices, there was discussion in 2005 on what should replace the legislation should a Labor Government come to power. Some, preferring a more militant approach, questioned the wisdom of relying on the federal Labor Party to overturn WorkChoices and restore lost conditions. Labor Leader Kim Beazley said that he would 'bin' the legislation but, as Ron McCallum observes, 'When institutions are destroyed or gutted or narrowed it's very hard to revive them' (McCallum, 2005).

Greg Combet caused some initial controversy in September when he suggested that unions would not necessarily advocate a return to the pre-1996 model (Hildebrand, 2005a). When the Clark Labour Government was elected in New Zealand in 1999, the union movement in New Zealand broadly concurred with the new Government's intention not to return to the arbitral model but to pursue a more union-friendly bargaining model and replace the viciously anti-union *Employment Contracts Act* with the *Employment Relations Act*. As in Australia, this may be effective for some sectors of the labour market, but not for unorganized, vulnerable workers or those whose wages and conditions are highly reliant on minimum standards. In industries where union membership is low, such as hospitality, Australian unions have relied almost wholly on awards to secure minimum conditions. The impact of WorkChoices in eroding conditions will be felt most keenly in these industries and could lead to a further weakening of union influence.

In September, a plenary discussion and workshop papers presented to the now biannual ACTU/New Zealand Council of Trade Unions Australasian Organizing Conference addressed the question. A common theme was that, rather than exacting revenge on business and political opponents when given the opportunity, the union movement should re-examine the industrial relations framework with international comparisons in mind. The union movement will need to consider whether to continue with the focus on enterprise bargaining or look for other means to deliver fairness in the workplace. In view of the real possibility of on-going conservative control of the Senate after the 2007 election, there will be ample time for debate until at least 2010.

Such a timeframe should at least allow unions the opportunity to develop a comprehensive and well-supported alternative, perhaps in contrast to their decision in the early 1990s to push for enterprise bargaining, an essentially hasty embracing of an alternative wages policy. It was the Business Council of Australia, however, that set the parameters of the debate about the shape enterprise bargaining would take (Briggs, 2001). The end result was that the union movement found itself ill-prepared and under-resourced at the workplace level where wages and working conditions would be determined.

Conclusion

The year 2005 was one in which unions were able to campaign around the issue of the WorkChoices legislation without being subject to it. In 2006 unions face the formidable tasks of continuing to win over public opinion, of finding innovative ways to organize and grow, of responding quickly to change, and of developing new IR policies as a political counter to those of the Howard Government. The degree to which unions are able to respond effectively to a hostile industrial framework and operate without recourse to the relatively accommodating arbitral model will perhaps determine which unions survive and which ones WorkChoices will have succeeded in neutering or destroying.

Although the 'Your Rights at Work' campaign very successfully generated public awareness and disquiet about the workplace reforms and contributed to a decline in support for the Government (Metherell, 2005a), it remains to be seen how unions will contest employers' application of the legislation. Greg Combet voiced one potential response at the November 15 rally, when he declared that 'I will not pay a $33,000 fine for demanding that someone be treated fairly – because the government has gone too far here…and I will be asking other union leaders to take a similar stance' (Workplace Express, 2005d).

The changed context in 2006 will undoubtedly constrain unions, but the potential erosion of wages and conditions may present them with opportunities to build on the successes of the rights at work campaign. The great threat, however, is that unions, confronted with declining membership, increased employer militancy and punitive legislation, will lack the resources (or the fortitude) to capitalize on the opportunities that present themselves.

Notes

1   In January 2006, the University of Ballarat required all new staff to sign an AWA rather than allowing them the option of coverage under an enterprise agreement.
2   The end of the Accord reduced the influence of peak councils and of the ACTU in particular. Historically, however, crises have galvanized and unified unions. The rights at work campaign witnessed a resurgence of unity of purpose within unions and the ACTU leadership. Unions embraced the campaign themes and adapted them for their own audiences. The need to fund the campaign resolved at least one contentious issue: the 2002 plans of the NSW Labor Council to sell Currawong had met with heated opposition, but the approval of its sale in late 2005 caused barely a stir, see Workers Online (2005c).
3   At the time of writing the picket line is still in place, as it has been since 2 June 2005.
4   The challenge confronting unions is to organize and seek to protect those who can no longer rely on benefits trickling down or on safety nets being in place. In the past unions have often not been successful in recruiting young people, but new initiatives are being tried. The Clara Weekes Project, initiated in 2003 by the Victorian Young Unionists Network and supported by the Victorian Trades Hall Council and several affiliates, blossomed in 2005. Young unionists visited more than 3000 students to inform them about their rights at work and unionism.
5   For details of the James Hardie issue, see Cooper (2005).

Acknowledgement

I would like to thank a number of unionists for their time and insights, in particular Brian Boyd, Sharan Burrow and Simon Cocker. I am also indebted to my colleagues and friends Chris Briggs, Paul Doughty, Diane Fieldes and Meg Smith for their comments on earlier drafts.

References

ABC Online (2005a) 'Union Warns IR Changes Threaten Australian Way of life', accessed 6 December 2005 http://www.abc.net.au/news/newsitems/200510/s1473030.htm
ABC Online (2005b) 'Union membership increases amidst IR changes', accessed 14 December 2005 http://www.abc.net.au/news/australia/qld/mackay/200511/s1500347
Auspoll (2005), 'State of The Union Report', prepared for Unions NSW, January.
Australian Bureau of Statistics (ABS) (2005) 'Employee Earnings, Benefits and Trade Union Membership Australia', Cat No. 6310.0, 22 March: 39.
Australian Council of Trade Unions (ACTU) (2005a) 'Sacked Mums go to Court over AWA's 25% Pay Cut', accessed 6 December 2005 http://www.actu.asn.au/public/news/1113968086_10548.html
Australian Council of Trade Unions (ACTU) (2005b) 'Advertising Campaign Puts Human Face to Work Changes', accessed 6 December 2005 http://www.actu.asn.au/public/news/1119139303_2893.html
Australian Council of Trade Unions (ACTU) (2005c) 'No Time for Games: Unions Reach Out to 300,000 AFL Spectators this Weekend', July 2005.
Australian Council of Trade Unions (ACTU) (2005d) 'Unions Win 2 Years Parental Leave and Right to PT Work For Working Parents', accessed 6 December 2005 http://www.actu.asn.au/public/news/1123467751_13914.html
Briggs, C. (2001) 'Australian Exceptionalism: The Role of Trade Unions in the Emergence of Enterprise Bargaining', *Journal of Industrial Relations* 43(1): 27–43.

Briggs, C. (2005) 'Industrial Relations: Secret Ballot or Secret War?', *Australian Policy Online*, accessed 5 January 2005 http://www.apo.org.au/webboard/results.chtml?filename_num=31147

Briggs C., Cooper, R. and Ellem, B. (2005) 'What About Collective Bargaining?' in Evatt Foundation, *The State of the States 2005, The State of Industrial Relations*, pp. 66–74. Sydney: Evatt Foundation.

Burrow, S. (2005) 'Address To International Labour Organisation', 10 accessed 5 January 2005 http://www.actu.asn.au/public/news/1118377855_18327.html

Cooper, R. (2005) 'Trade Unionism in 2004', *Journal of Industrial Relations* 47(2):208–9.

Crosby, M. (2005) *Power at Work. Rebuilding the Australian Union Movement.* Sydney: Federation Press.

Dabscheck, B. (1993) 'The Coaltition's Plan to Regulate Industrial Relations', *The Economic & Labour Relations Review* 4(1): 1–26.

Dyer, P. (2005) 'Reform Backlash – Rush to Sign Up for Unions', *Sunday Telegraph*, 13 November: 42.

Ellem, B. (2003) 'New Unionism in the Old Economy: Community and Collectivism in the Pilbara's Mining Towns', *Journal of Industrial Relations* 45(4): 423–41.

Gallaway, J. (2005) 'Back to the Future', interview with John Robertson, *Workers Online*, Issue 293: 20 December.

Gittens, R. (2005) 'The Changing Shape of Workplace Muscle', *Sydney Morning Herald*, 12 October: 17.

Hard Hat (2005a) CFMEU Construction & General Division national newspaper, September: 7.

Hard Hat (2005b) CFMEU Construction & General Division national newspaper, November/December: 3–6.

Hildebrand, J. (2005a) 'Combet's Challenge – Stand Up and Be Counted, Union Chiefs Told', *Daily Telegraph*, 12 September: 2.

Hildebrand, J. (2005b) 'Work Rule Changes to Cost Votes', *Daily Telegraph*, 28 September: 13.

Howard, J. (2005) doorstop media interview, Kirribilli House, 7 July.

Lewis, P. (2005) 'Editorial – Highway to help', *Workers Online*, Issue 282: 23 September.

LHMU (2005) 'Pink Salt Forks Out. Restaurant's E-mail Box Overloaded with Outraged Protests', media release, accessed 6 December 2005 http://www.lhmu.org.au/lhmu/news/1115348837_8614.html

McCallum, R. (2005) 'A Unique Attack on Workers' Rights', *Sydney Morning Herald*, 16 November: 15.

Marr, J. (2005) 'The Workers, United', *Workers Online*, July.

Metherell, M. (2005a) 'PM's Industrial Revolution Gets a Poll Shock', *Sydney Morning Herald*, 5 July: 1.

Metherell, M. (2005b) 'PM Firm on Battle of the Workplace', *Sydney Morning Herald*, 8 July: 10.

O'Malley, N, (2005a) 'Unions Face a Do-or-die Challenge', *Sydney Morning Herald*, 9 July: 35.

O'Malley, N. (2005b) 'Public Servants Warned off Mass Rally', *Sydney Morning Herald*, 5 November: 1.

O'Malley, N. and Metherell, M. (2005) 'Unions Shift Battle Plan for Howard Era', *Sydney Morning Herald*, 28 June: 1.

O'Malley, N. and Murphy, D. (2005) 'Given Their Marching Orders', *Sydney Morning Herald*, 19–20 November: 28.

Pocock, B. and Wright, P. (1997) 'Trade Unionism in 1996', *Journal of Industrial Relations* 39(1): 52–76.

Roy Morgan Research (2005) 'Morgan Poll: 2.5 million Australians Belong to a Trade Union – and a Further 1.5 Million Want to Join Them', 17 November accessed 5 December 2005 http://www.roymorgan.com/news/polls/2005/3928/index.cfm?printversion=yes

Workers Online (2005a) 'Last Weekend Gets a Lift', Issue 272: 15 July.

Workers Online (2005b) 'Masterton Homes Crumbles', Issue 273: 22 July.

Workers Online (2005c) 'Currawong Funds for IR Battle', Issue 290: 18 November.

Workers Online (2005d) 'Memberships on the Increase', Issue 291: 25 November.

Workplace Express (2005a) 'ACTU Launches $8m Advertising Campaign Against Second Wave', 19 June.

Workplace Express (2005b) 'NSW Unions Threaten to "Name and Shame" Rogue Employers', 1 July.

Workplace Express (2005c) 'ACTU Test Case on Work and Family', 8 August.

Workplace Express (2005d) 'Unions Promise Campaign of Civil Disobedience Against Second Wave', 15 November.

Workplace Express (2005e) 'Right to Request Provisions Finalised', 16 November.

7

Employer Matters in 2005

Bruce Hearn Mackinnon
Deakin University, Australia

Introduction

Previous reviews of employer matters have attempted to cover employer roles in important industrial disputes as well as in crucial AIRC hearings. Where possible, an attempt has been made to scan different industrial sectors and regions of the country in order to gain insights into the important position played by major employers as well by the major employer organizations. For this year's review, however, a more focused approach has been adopted. While some general commentary is included, the bulk of this review will focus on the role of a number of key employer organizations in both lobbying the Federal government to radically re-shape Australia's industrial relations regulatory regime, and in helping the government to sell its message of labour market reform to the general population.

Late in 2005 the Department of Employment and Workplace Relations' (DEWR's) chief counsel, James Smythe, revealed that the Federal government had seconded a number of lawyers from the country's biggest corporate law firms including Blake Dawson Waldron, Freehills, Clayton Utz, Phillips Fox, and Minter Ellison, to assist DEWR in drafting the WorkChoices legislation (Smythe, 2005). Thus, the lawyers representing the biggest corporations in Australia were involved first hand in drafting the government's new laws.

At the forefront of employer organization activism was the Business Council of Australia (BCA), representing the voice of big business, dominated by large mining and banking corporations. The country's most representative employer body, the Australian Chamber of Commerce and Industry (ACCI) also played a prominent role in promoting radical industrial relations reform, with support coming also from the manufacturing based Australian industry Group (AiG) and the staunchly conservative National Farmers Federation (NFF). Emboldened by its record of de-unionization since the early 1990s, the Australian Mines and Minerals Association (AMMA) focused its support for regulatory reform on the further weakening of protection for collective bargaining and the encouragement of common law agreements. By year's end, the far-right H R Nicholls Society was lambasting the Federal government for not going far enough in its reforms of the industrial relations system. An examination of the positions adopted by these major employer bodies now follows.

The BCA

As reported in last year's review (Hearn Mackinnon, 2005), the BCA had previously declared workplace relations to be one of its priority areas for attention in 2004 and 2005. True to its word, the BCA was the most pro-active of all employer organizations in supporting the Howard government's industrial relations reform package. Significant resources were devoted to building the case for further labour market reform, focusing on the supposed economic benefits, if not imperatives, of such reforms. In constructing the economic case for such reforms, the BCA commissioned the consultancy firm Access Economics to prepare a series of reports, which formed the basis of the BCA's position, which it advocated to the Federal government as well as to the community at large. In a very well planned exercise, these especially commissioned reports were released at 2–3 month intervals so as to maximize their cumulative impact on the government's industrial relations reform process.

The big business agenda for industrial relations reform was laid out early in the year with the release of the first of such commissioned reports, 'Workplace Relations – The Way Forward' (Access Economics, 2005a). This report formed the foundation for the BCA's 'Workplace Relations Action Plan' (BCA, 2005a) released simultaneously with the Access Economics report. The BCA action plan spelt out three clear objectives: greater flexibility in agreement making, reduced barriers to job creation and workforce participation, and more efficient workplace regulation.

To achieve greater flexibility in agreement making the plan proposed:

*   Reducing the allowable matters in Federal awards to cover only minimum rates of pay, sick leave, annual leave (excluding loadings), personal/carers leave, parental leave and dispute resolution. Over time the award system should be entirely replaced with a single set of minimum conditions.
*   Simplifying the no-disadvantage test applying to Australian Workplace Agreements (AWAs) and certified agreements by measuring them against six allowable award conditions only.
*   Simplifying the processing and approval of AWAs and extending their maximum life from three to five years.
*   Removing the automatic requirement for certification of collective agreements, and reducing the AIRC's role to that of checking that the agreement passes the no-disadvantage test. Providing parties with the option of having such agreements approved by either the AIRC or the Employment Advocate.

- Removing the AIRC's monopoly over conciliation and arbitration by establishing a statutory basis for the accreditation of private mediation service providers (BCA, 2005a: 9–14).

To achieve its second objective of reduced barriers to job creation and work-force participation, the BCA proposed:

- Removing the AIRC from having responsibility for maintaining the minimum wages safety net, by establishing a new board or committee with economic expertise which would make recommendations to the Federal government, focusing on the impact of any increases on the employment prospects of the unemployed.
- Reforming unfair dismissal laws to enable the identifying and filtering out of non-meritorious and frivolous claims. More broadly, the costs and benefits of Australia's unfair dismissal laws need to be examined with a view to further reform.
- The introduction of an earned income tax credit scheme to offset the barriers to workforce participation associated with effective marginal tax rates (BCA, 2005a: 151–8).

To help achieve its final objective of more efficient workplace regulation, the BCA proposed:

- The establishment of a single national system of workplace relations preferably via the voluntary referral of state powers to the Commonwealth. As a second best option, the BCA recommended the Federal government explore the use of its corporations power to achieve the 'broadest possible harmonization and ultimately a national, unitary system of workplace relations' (BCA, 2005a: 20).
- Compliance measures to be strengthened and streamlined to prevent unprotected industrial action and to assist businesses seeking damages where unprotected industrial action occurs. Protected action should be limited to ensure that businesses are not irreparably damaged, and special provisions and limits need to be imposed in the area of essential services.
- Ensuring that employment agreements should not transmit to an employer (who acquires a business) without the employer's agreement.
- Further consideration being given – especially in large enterprises with multi-union bargaining – to rationalizing representational rights in agreement making (BCA, 2005a: 21–22).

The BCA's action plan document also contained a case study, outlining the recent record of high productivity growth, high wages, wealth creation, strong investment and improved safety records pertaining to the mining sector, where around 50 percent of employees covered by Federal agreements are on AWAs, with some parts of the sector having AWA coverage as high as 80 percent (BCA, 2005a: 24–25).

To further strengthen the case for regulatory reform the BCA released two more reports commissioned by Access Economics, 'The Speed Limit' (Access

Economics, 2005b) and 'The Reform Dividend' (Access Economics, 2005c). In August the BCA released a document, 'Locking in or Losing Prosperity' (BCA, 2005b) based on the findings of the Access Economics reports. While these reports argued for a broad agenda of economic reform, including tax reform, investment and capital deepening, higher immigration, and improving the nation's education and training system, industrial relations reform was also highlighted as needing urgent attention if Australia's economic prosperity was to be protected and advanced.

The main argument advanced by the BCA was that 'fairness' should be removed as an objective of the nation's industrial relations' system. It argued that having fairness as the main objective of the system had held back the economic development of the country, and had not been effective in delivering fairness. Noting that Australia had 'focused its workplace relations policies on fairness rather than prosperity since the Harvester decision in 1907', it argued that this was problematic since minimum wages 'do next to nothing in alleviating poverty anyway' (Access Economics, 2005b: 23). Instead, 'fairness' should be left to the tax transfer system, with the industrial relations system being better directed towards promoting prosperity. In summary, the BCA's position was that 'it makes sense for the private sector to create wealth and for the public sector to redistribute it' (Access Economics, 2005b: 23).

In the face of a very effective public campaign by the Australian Council of Trade Unions (ACTU) opposing the Howard government's industrial relations reforms, the BCA committed millions of dollars to an advertising campaign aimed at shoring up support for the government's reform agenda. The money for the BCA campaign was raised from voluntary contributions of between $50,000 and $100,000 sought from its 100 members (Workplace Express, 2005a: 2).

In late October the BCA elected National Australia Bank (NAB) chair, Michael Chaney, as its new president for a two year term, replacing Hugh Morgan. The election of Chaney reflects the continued dominance of banking and mining corporations as the giants of the Australian economy. The other eight members of the BCA board include Philip Bulock (IBM CEO and managing director), Tony D'Aloisio (Australian Stock Exchange CEO), Geoff Dixon (Qantas CEO), Greig Gailey (Zinifex CEO), Angus James (ABN AMRO CEO), Katie Lahey (BCA chief executive), Charlie Lenegan (Rio Tinto managing director) and Rod Pearse (Boral CEO 7 managing director).

The ACCI

While the ACCI's position on workplace reform had certainly been well documented since the 2002 release of its 'Workplace Relations Blueprint' (ACCI, 2002), despite being the most representative of employer organizations, the ACCI was slow to develop its detailed case for workplace reforms, not releasing an issues paper until October and a position paper until November 2005.

In February, however, the ACCI provided strong support for the Federal government's right of entry bill, aimed at further restricting union access to Australian workplaces. According to the ACCI:

> Right of entry should only be exercised where employees choose to be represented by trade unions in respect of a particular workplace matter; such an approach is consistent with the principles of freedom of association ... [Furthermore, there is] ... nothing immutable or essential about trade union right of entry. Such provisions must be recognized for what they are – 'legalized trespass' in circumstances where that 'trespass' is considered justified as a matter of public policy. As such, the public policy case for trade union right of entry should apply to the minimum extent necessary to achieve that policy objective. (ACCI, 2005a)

In May the ACCI's chief executive, Peter Hendy, issued a press release supporting the Howard government's industrial relations reform package, and argued that 'the horse and buggy era for industrial relations is coming to an end ... [and] while there is still more to do, Australia will have moved from a 19th century system to one better suited to the 21st century'. Furthermore, he declared that the reforms 'if implemented, has the potential to kick-start a new round of productivity and employment growth in the private sector, and act as a foundation for higher living standards of families and for employment flexibility into the next decade' (ACCI, 2005b).

The ACCI issues paper put the case for the establishment of a unitary federal system of workplace regulations, based on five key conclusions:

- The establishment of a unitary federal system of labour law regulation, with appropriate checks and balances, is in the national interest and would enhance federalism.
- A unitary system of labour law regulation is consistent with the evolving nature of the Australian economy and society more generally.
- Implementing such a unitary system using existing Commonwealth powers is less than ideal, but is likely over time to meet the objectives of reform.
- The concept of competitive federalism has only limited relevance in the labour law context, and does not justify the retention of separate State systems.
- The State industrial systems cannot effectively act as a safe haven against Commonwealth governments making laws with respect to labour matters (ACCI, 2005c).

The ACCI's focus in the industrial relations debates of 2005 centered primarily on the need for a unitary federal system of labour law regulation. However, the position paper (ACCI, 2005d) it released in November, provided generalized support for the WorkChoices legislation, by arguing the economic case for such reforms.

The Howard government's reforms, according to the ACCI, would:

- reduce the incidence of joblessness, particularly for the most disadvantaged; and
- increase economic growth and productivity (ACCI, 2005d: 47).

Consequently, the ACCI argued that reform would increase wages, and with reduced joblessness, also reduce poverty. Furthermore, a less regulated economy would be more innovative, flexible, dynamic and better able to deal with shocks. To deal with current and future economic challenges, reform should occur now to:

- reduce the likelihood of an economic downturn; and
- to address the still excessively high levels of joblessness (ACCI, 2005d).

Summarizing its position, the ACCI paper concluded by confidently stating that:

> The economic case for labour market reform is profound, as are the economic and social benefits of reform in subsequent years and decades. The opportunities for reform presented by the *WorkChoices* package of November 2005, whatever its limitations, are there to be grasped, and in the national interest should be. (ACCI, 2005d)

The AiG

The AiG timed the release of its formal proposal (AiG, 2005) for industrial relations changes to coincide with the Federal government cabinet meeting at which Workplace Relations Minister, Kevin Andrews, tabled the detailed reform proposals.

Central to the AiGs proposals was the simplification of the award system, arguing for the reduction of the country's 2000 plus Federal awards to around 20. The industry sector system which previously operated in Victoria was held up as the model for a new simpler system. The rationalization of the award system would proceed by a specific timetable enshrined in legislation, after which only the 20 new awards would continue to be legally enforceable. Under the AiG proposal, the number of allowable matters in awards would be reduced from 20 to 10; achieved by removing some matters that have been legislated, rolling some together, and simply removing others (AiG, 2005: 33).

The AiG model also envisaged a new division of responsibilities between state and federal governments in providing a safety net of conditions. The federal government would maintain responsibility for governing termination of employment, including notice of termination, protection against unfair dismissal, exempting small business from paying severance, and unpaid parental leave; long service leave; and protection against sex, race, disability and age discrimination. To complement the role of the Federal government, the AiG model proposed that the states would in turn, maintain responsibility for legislating for occupational health and safety, equal employment opportunity, jury service and public holidays.

Interestingly, given the hostility toward the AIRC amongst the Federal government, the AiG argued for maintaining an important role for the AIRC, with the AiG stating that it should continue to maintain a 'substantial' part of the safety net, as 'the tribunal approach assists in ensuring a "fair go all round" and is likely to result in more consistency over time' (AiG, 2005).

Other key proposals by the AiG included:

- establishing a 'Minimum Wages Commission', modeled on the United Kingdom's 'Low Pay Commission'. It would make recommendations to the AIRC, which would then be precluded from awarding a higher increase than that recommended;
- beefing up the AIRC's powers to deal with pattern bargaining and 'damaging' industrial action and to oversee pre-strike secret ballots;
- barring provisions in awards and agreements that limit employers' ability to engage labour hire workers or contractors; and
- amending the *Cole Bill* to allow certification of project agreements for major construction projects.

The AiG also proposed extending the maximum allowable length of agreements from three to five years, simplifying the no-disadvantage-test and agreement approval processes, and ensuring parties genuinely try to reach agreement before being able to commence industrial action.

Once the details of the WorkChoices reforms were made public the AiG joined other employer groups in applauding the Federal government for its proposals, describing them as 'in sync with the needs of contemporary workplaces, the vast majority of which are operating in a highly competitive environment'. AiG chief executive, Heather Ridout said that while the AIRC's role would change, 'its importance to employers in the industries the Ai Group represents will remain critical. Ai Group welcomes the continued role of the AIRC in dispute resolution, facilitating genuine bargaining processes and maintaining the award safety net'. Pointedly, Ridout confessed that while the government's unfair dismissal changes went further than expected, they were 'clearly in response to the enormous frustration of Australian businesses with the operation of the existing laws' (Workplace Express, 2005b).

In addition to its general proposals for reforms, the AiG was particularly active in 2005 in lobbying the Federal government over its *Better Bargaining Bill*, which provided for lawful union bargaining to be stopped mid-dispute, as well as severely limiting unions' ability to pursue common claims. The AiG first lobbied the Federal government to introduce these reforms, aimed primarily at stamping out pattern bargaining, in the wake of the metal industry unions' Campaign 2003.

The AiG's Director – National Industrial Relations, addressing the Queensland Industrial Relations Society, described the new bargaining legislation as 'reasonable and practical'. Furthermore, he stated that 'this strong line is reasonable because protected industrial action was incorporated within the federal workplace relations system in 1993 for enterprise bargaining – not for industry bargaining disguised as enterprise bargaining, as pattern bargaining can be accurately described'. He went on to argue that the new laws posed no threats to parties engaging in genuine enterprise bargaining, but that 'they are clearly designed to stamp out coercion of companies to enter into union pattern agreements, and stamp out the refusal by some unions to deal with enterprise specific issues during bargaining' (Smith, 2005).

Highlighting why the rules for bargaining were of particular importance to members of the AiG, Smith stated that 70 percent of all federal certified agreements operated in the manufacturing and construction sectors (Smith, 2005).

The AMMA

The AMMA, arguably the employer organization most pro-active in promoting individual contracts or non-union collective agreements, made a number of important contributions to the industrial relations debates of 2005, by releasing a position paper in March, another in May, and then making two formal written submissions to the Senate's inquiry into the *WorkChoices Bill* in August and November.

In its position paper the AMMA began outlining its agenda by describing the success that employers in the mining sector have had since the 1980s in ridding their workplaces of union agreements. According to the paper, around 67 percent of mining sector employees covered by federal agreements are on AWAs, with the figure almost 80 percent in the metalliferous mining sector. A further 7 percent of these employees are covered by non-union collective agreements (AMMA, 2005a: 5). Pointing out that similar non-union arrangements dominate the property and business services sector as well as the hospitality industry, the AMMA declared:

> Notwithstanding this transformation of relationships between employers and employees in the majority of resources sector workplaces, Australia persists with its 100 year old patchwork of workplace laws and inefficient duplicate federal and state systems of industrial regulation. (AMMA, 2005a: 5)

In advocating a radical overhauling of Australia's industrial relations system, the AMMA proposed a two page *Contract of Employment Act*, included as an attachment to its position paper. Under this proposed act, the terms of contracts would be required to:

- exceed the scale of federally determined legislative terms and conditions;
- be in writing, and clearly identify the employer and employee;
- identify remuneration levels and how they are varied;
- specify pay periods and working time arrangements;
- specify entitlements to holidays, annual leave, long service leave and sick leave;
- specify notice periods for termination of employment contract, except for fixed term contracts where the expiry date must be specified; and
- list the employer's address and details of the workplace of the employee (AMMA, 2005a: 18).

The AMMA model provided that in return for meeting these above conditions, parties would be immune from any proceedings under federal or state industrial relations legislation, and that any enforcement of contracts made under the terms of the Act would be solely the domain of the courts. If an award system was to be maintained, then it should contain only the following seven allowable matters: four weeks annual leave (or cash out); one week sick leave; 52 weeks unpaid parental leave after 12 months service; a minimum weekly wage based on a 38-hour week; a minimum weekly wage for juniors based on a 38-hour week; a 'fair treatment' process; and an obligation to consult employees about change that might lead to redundancy (AMMA, 2005a: 8).

To narrowly define the parameters upon which the AIRC could exercise its award-making powers, the AMMA proposed that a template award be incorporated in the legislation, which the AIRC would be required to follow, except in setting rates of pay and classification structures appropriate to a particular industry or group of occupations. The AMMA also proposed:

- taking the issuing of s127 orders out of the AIRC's hands and giving them to the courts, and repealing s166A;
- providing courts the power to suspend union privileges – such as right of entry and representation on the particular project involved – where they defy orders to cease industrial action;
- outlawing any agreement provisions precluding the offering of AWAs, allowing AWAs to take effect as soon as they are signed, and confirming that AWAs cover the field on employment terms and conditions and over-ride state laws;
- giving the AIRC the power to suspend or end bargaining periods where industrial action affects projects or enterprises of 'significant national importance';
- making the certification of agreements a simple administrative function of either the Australian Industrial Registry or the OEA; and
- reducing the AIRC's compulsory arbitration functions (AMMA, 2005a: 9–19).

In May, the AMMA released another paper advocating a single national workplace relations system (AMMA, 2005b). The paper provided a range of examples of the apparent burden imposed upon employers by the existence of Australia's six separate statutory labour relations systems, arguably producing a very confusing industrial environment with considerable costly duplication.

In August, the AMMA made a Senate submission (AMMA, 2005c) containing much of the material outlined in the above mentioned position papers. This was followed up with a further Senate submission (AMMA, 2005d) in November. While generally pleased with the WorkChoices legislation, the AMMA argued for further amendments. In particular, it sought extending the unfair dismissal exemption to all businesses, providing for common law contracts to over-ride awards, extending the maximum term of union greenfields agreements to five years, treating old industrial agreements the same as 'pre-reform' agreements, and further tightening the s127 rules. The AMMA continued to argue for its model of internal regulation, first put forward in

2000 (AMMA, 2000), allowing workplaces to opt out of the traditional statu-tory based regulatory system in favour of self regulation.

In evidence during the last day of the WorkChoices inquiry, the AMMA's national industrial manager, Chris Platt, acknowledged that – contrary to gov-ernment rhetoric about employees bargaining directly with their employers – virtually no real bargaining took place in the non-collective stream, say-ing that employer greenfields agreements, which were written by employers, were similar in that regard to AWAs and common law contracts (Workplace Express, 2005c).

The NFF

The NFF was probably the least active of employer organizations, in terms of contributing to the industrial relations debates of 2005. Reflecting a sec-tor dominated by casual and seasonal labour, largely un-unionized, the NFF was not as pre-occupied with some of the issues of bargaining rules as other employer groups. While generally supportive of the WorkChoices reforms, however, the NFF was clearly frustrated at the constitutional limitations of the Commonwealth's jurisdiction based primarily on its corporations power. Given that around 90 percent of the NFF's farming members are unincor-porated, there was concern that they would fail to reap the benefits from the federal WorkChoices legislation, and instead become further subject to state awards. Not surprisingly, therefore, the NFF devoted much of their submis-sion to the Senate's WorkChoices inquiry, addressing the issues of a unitary system and the transitional arrangements for its implementation. In its submis-sion the NFF stated that:

> [The] NFF supports the concept of a unitary workplace system. However, the use of a variety of constitutional powers by the Federal Government, as opposed to a referral of industrial powers by the remaining State Governments, results in a limitation of the new system to achieve full unitary status. That is, certain businesses including a large number of farming businesses are not covered under the constitutional powers utilised to underpin the reforms. (NFF, 2005)

In the absence of any likelihood of the remaining states referring their indus-trial relations powers to the Commonwealth, the NFF was generally pleased with the transitional arrangements put in place by the Federal Government. Under the transitional arrangements for federal award coverage, any unincor-porated business (hence, not subject to the WorkChoices legislation) currently operating under a federal award, will continue to maintain federal award cov-erage for a period of five years. Such a five year transition period will provide most farming businesses time to determine whether to incorporate, all or part of their business.

The NFF submission also said that it expected there would be a large take up by farmers of workplace agreements under the WorkChoices system, but that these were more likely to be collective agreements, which were easier to introduce. Due to the use of casual and seasonal employment, many farmers were likely to continue to rely on awards, rather than workplace agreements. Finally, recognizing the apparent unpopularity of the WorkChoices reforms amongst the wider community, the NFF argued that the government needed to devote significant resources to an education campaign to inform all Australians about the reforms (NFF, 2005: 15).

The MBA

Cracks amongst employer ranks, and between them and the Federal government, were revealed in a submission the Master Builders Association (MBA) delivered to the Workplace Relations Minister, Kevin Andrews, concerning the *Building and Construction Industry Improvement Bill* (BCII Bill) and the future of workplace relations. Whereas, most other employer organizations, especially the AiG and the ACCI, wanted strong government legislation to stamp out 'pattern bargaining', the MBA was under pressure from its own membership to ensure a 'level playing field'. Given the nature of the building and construction industry, with very little continuous employment, genuine enterprise-by-enterprise bargaining would result in continuous disruption on projects. It was perhaps not surprising, therefore, that there appeared to be a growing view amongst many building and construction employers that the Government legislation was too ideological. As consultant Tony Mussert put it, the 'ideologues – much as I love them' – would create 'commercial stupidity' if they got their way (Workplace Express, 2005d).

According to the MBA's Victorian industrial relations manager, Lawrie Cross, the MBA, while generally supportive of the vast bulk of the government's legislation, was concerned about some of its provisions, particularly the pattern bargaining injunctions. Instead, the MBA was more concerned that there be a more stringent test to ensure that agreements were genuinely entered into (Workplace Express, 2005d).

The MBA submission acknowledged that many of the provisions of the BCII Bill ran counter to the more decentralized workplace relations system employers and the government were championing. Due to the activities of militant construction unions, the MBA argued for more regulation of the building and construction industry to restore the 'rule of law' (Workplace Express, 2005d: 3–4). Nevertheless, the MBA also argued that some of this regulation should also be incorporated into wider industrial relations law.

The MBA faced a dilemma early in 2005, with building and construction unions, chiefly the Construction Mining Forestry and Energy Union (CFMEU), seeking to 'go early' and negotiate new deals with employers before the government's new tougher legislation came into force. Initially the MBA, with urging from the Federal government, advised its members to resist the union's proposals, and instead, wait until the BCII Bill was law, whereupon employers' powers would be considerably enhanced.

Despite the pressuring from the Federal government, and advice of the MBA, in March a group of builders in Victoria reached an in-principle agreement with the CFMEU on a new three-year agreement, which provided workers with a 13 percent wage increase and a 36 hour week with 26 rostered days off (RDOs) (Workplace Express, 2005e). By June, employers in most other states had reached or were negotiating similar deals with the CFMEU. In early July, the MBA of Victoria (MBAV) – after learning that one of the industry's major contractors had successfully lobbied the DEWR and gained Code compliance approval – did an 'about face' by reversing its previously strong opposition to the deal. In negotiations with the CFMEU, the MBA extracted some concessions, including the exclusion of the housing industry from the deal, and less onerous requirements on redundancy, sick leave and apprentices' superannuation. The substantial components of the deal, however, remained unchanged.

In a briefing to its members, the MBAV acknowledged that despite its opposition, the CFMEU had been successful in signing up contractors and sub-contractors to its new deal, by declaring that 'given this reality, and the fact that in excess of 500 companies had signed the CFMEU EBA, the MBAV reasoned that the longer the CFMEU document remained unchallenged – the more likely it was to become feted as the industry standard' (Workplace Express, 2005f). Soon after, similar agreements had been negotiated in other states, meaning that building and construction employers had successfully negotiated new enterprise agreements with the CFMEU, without suffering the usual round of industrial disputation.

The Last Safety Net Review?

In what is likely to be the Commission's last national wage case hearing, in response to the ACTU's $26.60 'Living Wage' claim, the Australian Chamber of Commerce and Industry (ACCI) supported a $10 increase, while the Australian industry Group (AiG) and the Federal Government supported an $11 increase. The only difference between the positions of the two major employer groups was that the ACCI argued for a $10 increase up to the C10 tradesperson's classification, while the AiG backed an $11 increase for all awards. The federal government also supported the increase being limited to the C10 classification in the metals award. This broadly common position of the ACCI and AiG was almost identical to their positions in 2004, but in contrast to 2003 when the AiG supported an $11 increase, while the ACCI argued for no increase at all.

It was perhaps surprising to find the Federal government and the major employer organizations arguing for increases in the award safety net, while simultaneously proposing to end the AIRC's role in adjusting minimum wages, in part because they had raised the safety net too high, the effect being to price workers out of jobs. A more logical and consistent position would have been for the Howard government and employer groups to have been regular opponents of any increase in the safety net. Yet they found themselves arguing in one arena that the current safety net was too high, yet before the AIRC they supported a small increase in the same safety net. In any event, on 7 June 2005 the

AIRC awarded a $17-a-week increase for all award classifications, only slightly below its record $19 increase awarded in 2004 (AIRC, 2005).

Conclusion

By any yardstick one cares to apply, employer organizations were enormously successful in 2005 in getting the Federal government to adopt the reforms to industrial relations law they had long advocated. The public relations battle was a different matter altogether, with the ACTU media campaign proving to be enormously successful in generating public opposition to the Government's WorkChoices laws. Despite a massive publicity campaign run by the Federal government and supported by major employer groups, late in 2005 a Roy Morgan poll revealed that only 17 percent of people agreed with the new labour laws, while 49 percent disagreed with the changes (Roy Morgan Research, 2005).

Nevertheless, with these laws finally enacted, 2006 may well come to be known as 'year zero', the date from which a whole new 'ball game' comes into play. Obviously, with looming High Court challenges, and continued resistance from the states, only time will tell how successful the WorkChoices reforms turn out to be, but at the time of writing it was hard to imagine any employer organizations being disappointed with the outcomes of 2005.

At year's end, the main issues of concern amongst employer organizations were the limitations of the WorkChoices legislation, based on the Commonwealth's corporations power in the constitution, in being able to establish a truly unitary regulatory regime for industrial relations. There were signs of some continued unease with the Federal government's apparent ideological fixation with enterprise-by-enterprise bargaining amongst employers in the building and construction industry, but armed with the tougher provisions of the BCII Bill, employers will not be able to blame the law if they are unable to make the industrial relations reforms work to their advantage in coming years.

Just when one might have expected celebrations from all employer groups at their victory in reforming the industrial relations system, the year closed with the far-right H R Nicholls Society attacking the Federal government for weakness, resulting from 'its continuing acceptance of the Marxist dogmas which inspired the trade union movement of the 1880s and 1890s, and their contemporary supporters from the intellectual classes' (Evans, 2005). It just goes to show, you can't please everyone!

References

Access Economics Pty Ltd (2005a) 'Workplace Relations – The Way Forward', report commissioned by the Business Council of Australia, 15 February.
Access Economics Pty Ltd (2005b) 'The Speed Limit 2005–2025', report commissioned by the Business Council of Australia, May.

Access Economics Pty Ltd (2005c) 'The Reform Dividend 1983–2004', report commissioned by the Business Council of Australia, July.

Australian Industry Group (AiG) (2005) 'Making the Australian Economy Work Better', Workplace Relations, 6 March.

Australian Chamber of Commerce and Industry (ACCI) (2002) 'Modern Workplace: Modern Future 2002–2010', Policy Blueprint.

Australian Chamber of Commerce and Industry (ACCI) (2005a) Submission to the Right of Entry legislation inquiry, February.

Australian Chamber of Commerce and Industry (ACCI) (2005b) 'Business Welcomes Industrial Relations Joining the 21st Century – Reform Detail will be Crucial', Press Release, 26 May.

Australian Chamber of Commerce and Industry (ACCI) (2005c) 'Functioning Federalism and the Case for a National Workplace Relations System', Issues Paper, October.

Australian Chamber of Commerce and Industry (ACCI) (2005d) The Economic Case for Workplace Relations Reform, Position Paper, November.

Australian Industrial Relations Commission (AIRC) (2005) Safety Net Review – Wages, PR002005, 7 June.

Australian Mines & Minerals Association (AMMA) (2000) 'A Model of Internal Regulation of Employee Relations', Discussion Paper, February.

Australian Mines & Minerals Association (AMMA) (2005a) 'AMMA Position Paper on Workplace Relations Legislative Reform Options', 10 March.

Australian Mines & Minerals Association (AMMA) (2005b) 'AMMA Position Paper on the Requirement for a Single National Workplace Relations System', 18 May.

Australian Mines & Minerals Association (AMMA) (2005c) 'AMMA Submission to Senate Employment, Workplace Relations and Education Legislative Committee: Inquiry on Workplace Agreements', 4 August.

Australian Mines & Minerals Association (AMMA) (2005d) 'AMMA Submission to Senate Employment, Workplace Relations and Education Legislative Committee: Inquiry into Workplace Relations Amendment' (WorkChoices) Bill 2005, 18 November.

Business Council of Australia (BCA) (2005a) 'Workplace Relations: Action Plan for Future Prosperity', 15 February.

Business Council of Australia (BCA) (2005b) Locking in or Losing Prosperity: Australia's Choice, August.

Evans, N. R. (2005) 'President's Report', H R Nicholls Society 2005 Annual General Meeting, 5 December.

Hearn Mackinnon, B. (2005) 'Employer Matters in 2004', *Journal of Industrial Relations* 47(2): 212–25.

National Farmers Federation (NFF) (2005) NFF Submission to the Inquiry into the Workplace Relations Amendment (WorkChoices) Bill 2005, 10 November.

Roy Morgan Research (2005) 'Opinions Unchanged After Massive Publicity and Debate on Industrial Relations Reforms – Only 10% Say They'll be Better Off', Finding No. 3909, 18 October http://www.roymorgan.com/news/polls/polls.cfm

Smith, S. (2005) 'Reasonable Rules or Rafferty's Rules?', Speech to the Queensland Industrial Relations Society Conference, Gold Coast, 22 September.

Smythe, J. (2005) As reported in Proof Committee Hansard, Senate, Commonwealth of Australia, 'Employment, Workplace Relations and Education Legislative Committee – Estimates', 3 November: 106.

Workplace Express (2005a) 'BCA Asks Members for Money', 11 October.

Workplace Express (2005b) 'Bleak Future for Workers, Say Unions, while Business Welcomes Change', 26 May.

Workplace Express (2005c) 'AMMA Calls for Further Changes to Work Choices', 18 November.

Workplace Express (2005d) 'Government Says Cole Bill Won't be Amended, as Vic Bargaining for Early Deal Continues', 21 January.

Workplace Express (2005e) 'Victorian Construction Employers Defy Government and Reach Agreement', 17 March.

Workplace Express (2005f) 'MBAV Goes with the Flow on Early CFMEU Deal', 4 July.

8

Recent Industrial Relations Developments in the United Kingdom: Continuity and Change under New Labour 1997–2005

David Nash
Cardiff Business School, UK

Introduction

With Labour's election victory in 2005, Tony Blair achieved his ambition of being the first Labour Prime Minister to serve two consecutive full terms in office. This milestone also provides commentators with an opportunity to reflect on the achievements of the past eight years. Scholars in the field of industrial relations have been more interested than most in debating the characteristics of New Labour and the extent to which it has marked a break with the past or a continuation of the policies of its Conservative predecessors. The terms of debate can be seen to centre on the areas of individual and collective regulation of the employment relationship and the extent to which the government has encouraged a more partnership-oriented approach to industrial relations. It will be argued that in all of these areas New Labour's interventions have been contradictory and incoherent.

The field of individual employment law has certainly been changed since 1997. Various policy developments have extended new protections to individual employees in the areas of minimum wages and working time. There have also been developments in the areas of discrimination and protection from employer exploitation (Dickens and Hall, 2003). Critics of the government have highlighted the weakness of many of the legislative provisions, however. This has been epitomized in the minimal implementation of the various directives to come out of Europe, where the government has either negotiated various 'opt outs' to dilute the efficacy of the policies or refused to sign up at all. Such an approach is highlighted by Waddington (2003) who cites the government's refusal to award legal status to the EU's Charter of Fundamental Rights.

Collective employment law has seen no less change in the eight years since

Labour came to power. The most significant development in this area has been the creation of a statutory recognition procedure for trade unions under the provisions of the 1999 Employment Relations Act. It has been claimed that this represents a key change in government policy and puts unions on a legal footing akin to that in the 1970s. Supporters claim that it is not so much the statutory procedure itself but its shadow that has granted unions greater legitimacy and encouraged significant numbers of employers to enter into voluntary recognition agreements (Wood and Godard, 1999). A more critical appraisal of the government's record would highlight that there has been more continuity than change, however. Critics point to the fact that the majority of the Conservative legislation of the 1980s and 90s that curtailed the power of unions to go on strike and prescribed much of their internal operation has been retained by New Labour.

It has been argued that the most significant break with the previous 18 years of Conservative government has been the move towards a model of social partnership. The inclusion of trade unionists on public bodies such as the Low Pay Commission and the Central Arbitration Committee have been cited as important both for their symbolism and for the operation of the institutions in question (Brown, 2000; Metcalf, 1999). Writers sympathetic to Labour also cite the encouragement for firm level labour–management partnerships by both the TUC and the government. However, critics argue that both forms of partnership are more 'style' than 'substance'. At the macro level it is argued that the inclusion of union interests has been more than offset by the government's attempts to assuage the concerns of the business community (McIlroy, 2000). Similarly, partnership agreements between individual unions and firms have been dismissed as symptomatic of a weakened trade union movement, which is obliged to align its interests with those of the employers (Charlwood, 2004).

This article will outline the legislative developments of the Labour government in more detail, looking at the aforementioned three areas of individual and collective employment law and partnership. It will go on to assess the overall impact of the government's industrial relations programme in the context of the wider debate between those who argue that Britain is becoming more European on the one hand, and more Americanized on the other. The review will conclude that it is too simplistic to argue that New Labour is either a continuation of the past or constitutes a radical recasting of the industrial relations landscape in Britain.

Developments in Individual Employment Regulation

The introduction of a national minimum wage represented a significant change in British labour market policy, especially in comparison to that of the previous Conservative administrations. Some form of statutory wage regulation existed in Britain for most of the last century. Both the Fair Wage Resolutions (FWR) that were introduced in 1891 and the system of Wages Councils, which started to appear in 1909 and reached a peak of 3.5 million workers in the 1950s

(Metcalf, 1999: 172) provided wage protection to low paid workers. Under the Conservative government of 1979 the Wages Councils lost much of their significance and were finally abolished in 1993. Support for some form of minimum wage gained ground in the mid 1980s with the trade union movement and then the Labour Party advocating the introduction of a comprehensive system of wage protection.

The election of the New Labour government in May 1997 was swiftly followed by the creation of the Low Pay Commission (LPC), a tri-partite body of union representatives, figures from industry and independent academic experts under the chairmanship of George Bain. The LPC was initially charged with recommending the initial level of the minimum wage, together with any exemptions or lower rates for those aged 16–25 (Metcalf, 1999). This role was later amended to include the monitoring and evaluation of the effects of the minimum wage. The recommendations of the LPC were largely accepted by the government and came into force on 1st April 1999. The minimum wage for adults was set at £3.60 per hour with a lower rate of £3.00 for those aged 18–21 or those on approved training courses (for a full description of the provisions of the regulations see Metcalf, 1999). The minimum wage has subsequently been up-rated and since 2003 these increases have outstripped the rise in the Average Earnings Index (AEI) over the same period (Metcalf, 2004: C85). In 2004 the minimum wage was extended to cover 16–17 year olds at a lower rate of £3.00 per hour. As of October 2005 the minimum wage is £5.05 for adults with a youth and development rate of £4.25.

The effects of the minimum wage are still the subject of investigation and debate. Research undertaken when the regulations came into force in 1999 estimated it had resulted in an average increase in pay of 30 percent for nearly two million workers (9 percent of the workforce) at a cost to the national pay bill of about 0.6 percent (Metcalf, 1999). Of those benefiting from the new minimum wage, 60 percent were female and 70 percent were part-time. A related intervention in the labour market was the introduction of the Working Families Tax Credit, which was designed to guarantee a minimum net income to low wage households and encourage people into work and off state benefits. Evidence suggests that the policy had the effect of encouraging 25,000 lone parents into work during the first nine months of its operation (Hamann and Kelly, 2003: 646). This, combined with the introduction of the lower band of income tax of 10 percent, has significantly increased the earnings of the lowest decile. However, research seems to show that the redistributive effect of the minimum wage has not been felt higher up the earnings distribution (Low Pay Commission, 2003).

The feared unemployment inducing effects of the minimum wage seem not to have materialized (Stewart, 2004). Even previously low paying parts of the economy, such as the aged care sector where 40 percent of staff were being paid below £3.60 when the minimum wage was introduced in 1999, only experienced weakly negative employment effects (Machin and Wilson, 2004). Another area of concern prior the introduction of the minimum wage was the effect it would have on training of less skilled workers. Human capital theory predicts that in competitive labour markets the introduction of a minimum wage will prevent workers being able to finance their training through the acceptance of lower wages. However, in a recent study using data from the British Household Panel Survey Arulampalam et al. (2004) found that the probability of training incidence and training intensity increased by 8 percent–11 percent for those workers affected by the minimum wage. Thus, whilst the empirical studies seem to show that the minimum wage has had a benign effect, some have argued that this is a reflection of the fact that the rates are set too low.

A policy intervention as potentially significant as the minimum wage was that surrounding working time. Historically the UK had no system of working time regulation. During the 1980s any protection that had existed, such as the Wages Councils ability to regulate working hours and paid holidays, was removed by successive Conservative governments (Hall and Sisson, 1997). John Major's government had challenged the legal basis of the European Working Time Directive that had been enacted in 1993, a challenge that was finally rejected by the European Court of Justice in 1996. Thus, when Labour came to power the following year, they inherited the directive which finally came into force in 1998. Britain, for the first time, had a comprehensive legal framework that regulated issues relating to working time. The directive had provisions on a broad range of working time issues. The most well known of the provisions is a limit of 48 hours on the average working week (measured over a four month cycle). There are also entitlements to a rest period after six hours continuous work, and workers should receive a minimum of 11 hours rest in any 24 hour period (over a two week reference period). More controversial provisions included a stipulated minimum of four weeks annual paid leave with no opting-out (Adnett and Hardy, 2003: 116). There are also restrictions on the amount of night work that workers should be exposed to.

However, the implementation of the working time directive has been weakened in the UK by a complex system of 'derogations' and exceptions. The directive can be implemented more flexibly where there is a collective agreement with a trade union or a 'workforce agreement' with elected employee representatives (Dickens and Hall, 2003). Perhaps more significantly, individual employees are able to 'opt out' of the 48-hour limit on the working week, although employers are obliged to keep records of working hours and must not subject employees to any detriment for refusing to work longer hours (Adnett and Hardy, 2003: 115).

The Labour government has also reversed the narrowing of coverage of existing protections that was characteristic of the previous Conservative administrations. Many of these extended rights were enshrined in the Employment Relations Act 1999. The qualification period for a number of employment rights (such as unfair dismissal) was reduced to one year. This change extended protection from unfair dismissal to an extra one to two million workers (Hamann and Kelly, 2003). Other changes made it illegal to include clauses in fixed-term contracts that exempt employees from unfair dismissal protection (Dickens and Hall, 2003). Under the provisions of the *Part-Time Workers (Prevention of Less Favourable Treatment) Regulations* 2000, part-time workers were to have the right to be treated equally with their full-time counterparts in the same employment (Brown, 2000). However, this restricted basis for comparison has had the effect of excluding the majority of part time workers from the provisions of the regulations because there were often no comparable full-time workers in the same employment (McKay, 2001). The maximum fines payable by employers found guilty of unfair dismissal has also been increased from £12,000 to £50,000 and was also index linked to maintain its real value into the future. Significantly, the ceiling on compensation awards in cases of discrimination has been removed.

Legislation in the area of equality has been largely driven by the need to implement EU directives. The *Employment Framework Directive* was agreed in October 2000, and stated that member states should have legislation in place outlawing discrimination based on sexual orientation and religion by 2003 and on age and disability by 2006 (McKay, 2001). Further improvements were made in the area of disability discrimination by widening the scope of the 1995 legislation to include smaller firms and by establishing a Disability Rights Commission of equivalent status to the existing commissions for equal opportunities and racial equality respectively. The *Race Relations Act* was amended to oblige public bodies to promote race equality in their operations (Dickens and Hall, 2003). However, there was no radical overhaul of the framework of race or sex discrimination law following Labour's assumption of power.

An area in which the Labour government sought to mark itself as distinct from its predecessors was that of equality. This was closely linked with the rise in so called 'family-friendly' or 'work–life balance' policies. Much of the legislative programme surrounding equality has been driven by the European Union. The provisions of the EU *Parental Leave Directive* were assimilated into UK law by the *Maternity and Parental Leave Regulations* in 1999. This gave new entitlements to parental leave and for time off due to family emergencies. The family friendly agenda has been further strengthened by the *Employment Act* 2002 which introduced new statutory rights on paternity leave and pay, lengthened the period over which maternity pay was paid and granted greater flexibility to those with child-care responsibilities (Waddington, 2003).

Changes in Collective Employment Rights

The flagship piece of legislation in Labour's first term was the 1999 Employment Relations Act (ERA). The most noteworthy provision of the act was the reintroduction of a statutory union recognition procedure. However, there were a number of other provisions that were also designed to be beneficial to trade unions. Blacklists held by employers about union activists were outlawed and it was also made illegal to dismiss such activists. Union members undertaking lawful industrial action were also protected from dismissal during the first eight weeks of such action. Giving preferential terms and conditions to non-union members was outlawed by the act and obstacles were put in the way of employer victimization by removing the requirement that unions give employers the names of those who were balloted in relation to industrial action. The requirement for a ballot on the subject of the deduction of union dues from payroll, so called 'check-off', was scrapped altogether. Finally, the act abolished the office of the Commissioner who had the dual responsibility for the protection of union members (CRTUM) and for protection against unlawful industrial action (CPAUIA), roles that Brown (2000: 302) suggests offered a form of 'legal aid' to union members seeking to take action against their unions.

The most significant provision of the act was that which dealt with statutory union recognition. The ERA provided a procedure by which unions could attain recognition from an employer for the purposes of collective bargaining (over pay, hours and holiday entitlements), even in the face of employer opposition. This effectively sought to reverse the provisions of Conservative legislation of the 1980s and early 1990s whereby the decision to bargain collectively with a trade union was given to the employer, irrespective of the level of union membership and support. Whilst undoubtedly signifying a break with the past, the terms of the recognition procedure fell well below what unions had hoped for and granted employers more influence over the process than had been expected.

The most straightforward cases of recognition were those in which unions could demonstrate that a majority of the bargaining unit were members. In such cases, recognition would be automatic. The newly formed Central Arbitration Committee (CAC) had a role to play in that it was responsible for defining the bargaining unit in cases where employer and union could not agree and it could insist a ballot be held in those workplaces with majority union membership if it suspected that such support was weak or recent (Howell, 2004: 10). In the more usual situation where a union (or group of unions if applying together) could not demonstrate majority membership a ballot is required. For an application to be accepted by the CAC the union needs to demonstrate a minimum threshold membership of 10 percent of the proposed bargaining unit. For recognition to be granted a majority of those voting and over 40 percent of those eligible to vote must be attained. This 'majoritatian principle' contrasts to the approach taken in the 1970s, which was more concerned with whether there was enough support to make collective bargaining viable, acknowledging the beneficial effect that employer recognition can have on union membership (Dickens and Hall, 2003: 138).

Despite broad support for the ERA there are also perceived weaknesses. First amongst these is the fact that its provisions only apply to those firms with over 20 employees, thereby excluding a quarter of employees from the recognition procedure (Wood and Godard, 1999). Similarly the means of enforcement have caused confusion and concern. In the event of an employer refusing to bargain after recognition has been imposed upon them the union may apply to the courts for an order compelling the employer to act as required (so called 'specific performance'). Failure to comply with such an order could in theory lead to criminal sanctions (Dickens and Hall, 2003). Again, this contrasts with the approach taken in the 1970s whereby an industrial settlement was imposed by arbitration (Brown, 2000). At the time, many argued that the compliance procedure embodied in the ERA was overly legalistic and would lead to uncertainty and controversy (Hepple, 2000), although this seems to not have materialized in the years since the introduction of the regulations.

The efficacy of the ERA in promoting union recognition should be measured both directly and indirectly. After nearly three years of the Act operating, the CAC reported 255 applications being made, with recognition being granted in 58 cases, 23 of which required no ballot (Howell, 2004: 10). This relatively modest total is offset by the rise in voluntary recognition agreements that have been concluded since the act came into force. In fact, the mere spectre of a statutory recognition procedure had a noticeable effect on employers with the TUC reporting 74 new recognition agreements, covering more than 21,000 workers, in the first 10 months of 1999, with more than half being employer instigated. This represented a more than doubling of the figure for the preceding year (Brown, 2000: 303). Howell further points out that cases of union derecognition were declining prior to the implementation of the ERA, suggesting that the industrial relations climate may have been thawing as the legislation loomed (Howell, 2004).

The impact of the ERA on union recognition is not confined to the effect of the procedure outlined above. The legislation also established a statutory right for a worker to be accompanied by a trade union official at disciplinary or grievance proceedings. It has been argued (Brown, 2000; Dickens and Hall, 2003) that such a provision could be as significant for union expansion as the formal recognition procedure. Under the rights of accompaniment set out under the ERA a union official has the right to attend a disciplinary or grievance hearing where invited to do so by workers. These workers need not necessarily be members of a union and this right applies even in cases where unions are not recognized by the employer. Furthermore, firms of 20 or fewer employees are covered even though they are excluded from the formal recognition procedure. Brown argues that this access to employees could provide fertile ground for union recruitment given that in the private sector only eight percent of workers in firms employing fewer than 25 people are members of a union (Brown, 2000: 303).

Potentially more significant than any of the domestically enacted industrial relations legislation since 1997 is the adoption of EU directives that create a dual channel of representation in Britain. The European Works Councils (EWC) directive was passed in 1994, but only finally introduced in the UK in 2000. Under the provisions of the directive EWCs were to be created in 'Community-scale' undertakings, which were defined as those organizations that had over 1000 employees within the EU, including at least 150 in each of two (or more) member states. The directive stipulated that the EWCs be consulted about decisions that affected the organization as a whole, including those relating to relative resource allocations between the various establishments. At the time of implementation the Department for Trade and Industry estimated that 230 UK-based multinationals would be subject to the EWC directive (Terry, 2003: 276). The European Trade Union Institute reported that 95 of these had created EWCs by 2001 (Terry, 2003: 276). Thus the impact of the EWC directive has been largely symbolic. The labour government was able to reverse the previous administration's decision to opt out of the regulations without fear of fundamentally changing the nature of industrial relations landscape.

By contrast, the new government was far more worried about the system of national works councils that would be set up under the provisions of the EU Information and Consultation Directive. Tony Blair had led opposition to the proposals, whilst the TUC had openly supported them, citing the example of Vauxhall's decision to close its Luton plant at the cost of thousands of jobs as evidence of the need for works councils. After negotiation over the phasing in of the provisions of the directive, it was transposed into British Law in 2003. The phased introduction meant that the regulations would cover establishments of more than 150 employees in 2005, those with 100 or more employees in 2007 and finally in 2008 the UK would be brought into line with the rest of the EU with establishments of more than 50 employees being covered. The new works councils were to have rights of information on the general economic situation and development of the business and consultation rights in the areas of employment levels, work organization and proposed structural change of the business. Crucially, however, the councils were not granted any rights of codetermination, thus rendering them impotent when compared to their more established cousins in continental Europe. It is too early to evaluate the effects of having a statutory second channel of representation in Britain and whether it will be merely symbolic, or will fundamentally change the industrial relations landscape.

The Move Towards Partnership

A further area of change in Labour's industrial settlement centres on the emergence of the notion of partnership. This has been examined at the level of the relationship between individual management and unions and at the wider macro level. The 1999 TUC publication *Partners for Progress: New Unionism at the Workplace* advocated industrial partnership at individual enterprise level (Brown, 2000). This acted as a type of blueprint that spelled out what the TUC considered to be the prerequisites for a successful partnership agreement. Six principles were identified. First, there should be shared commitment to the business goals of the organization. Second, there should be a recognition and acceptance of the fact that the two parties in the partnership may hold different interests, and that these interests should be legitimately represented. Third, measures to increase flexibility of labour use should not be at the expense of employees' security and this should be maintained by maximizing the transferability of skills and experience within the organization. Fourth, partnership should positively encourage the personal development of employees, through training programmes. Fifth, the relationship between management and the union should be based on open and informed consultation. Lastly, the partnership agreement should add value to the business by increasing the level of employee motivation in the workplace.

This notion of labour–management partnership was enthusiastically promoted by the government. Wood (2000) argues that central to the government's understanding of partnership is a notion of 'high involvement HRM' that is designed to increase worker motivation with the goal of raising quality and productivity. Under the provisions of the ERA the Department for Trade and Industry set up a Partnership at Work Fund to give training to companies wishing to enter into a partnership agreement. Charlwood (2004) claims that whilst this may have been useful in helping companies who had already decided to go down that route, it is unlikely to have attracted many non-partnership companies into adopting that approach. Indeed according to TUC figures, only 80 organizations had adopted a union based partnership agreement by October 2002 (Waddington, 2003: 347). The significance of labour–management partnership has also been debated. Despite some high profile successes, such as the Union of Shop, Distributive and Allied Workers (USDAW) claiming an increase in membership of 20,000 in the first year of their partnership with Tesco, Waddington (2003: 347) reports there appears to be no significant link between partnership and rising union density. Indeed, despite government exhortations about the importance of partnership agreements, there is nothing in their stated conception of partnership that requires unions to be involved (Howell, 2004; Waddington, 2003).

It is perhaps in the wider notion of partnership that the Labour government has distinguished itself from its predecessors. After nearly two decades of being excluded from the policy-making process, some commentators have argued that New Labour have brought unions in from the cold and have moved some way towards the model of social partnership that is characteristic of many industrial relations systems in continental Europe. An example of this shift is the Low Pay Commission that was created by the government within months of coming to power in 1997. Both Brown (2000) and Metcalf (1999) claim that the operation of the LPC constitutes a form of 'social partnership'. The composition of the commission certainly seems to support this view. Of the nine commissioners, three have trade union backgrounds and three come from industry. Brown (2000) argues that the fact that these members are closely linked to the TUC and CBI respectively adds legitimacy to the work of the LPC. Further examples of such tri-partite bodies could be the council of the Advisory, Conciliation and Arbitration Service (ACAS) and the newly formed Central Arbitration Committee (CAC). It is difficult to argue, however, that these institutions constitute an embrace of the notion of social partnership in its fullest sense. The recommendations of the LPC, whilst largely being accepted by the government were disappointing to many in the labour movement, who had been campaigning for a far higher level than half male median earnings (Metcalf, 1999: 173). Similarly, many on the left felt that ACAS had been emasculated by the removal of its mandate to promote collective bargaining in 1983 and were bitterly disappointed by the Labour government's refusal to restore it (Hyman, 2003: 55). The desire of the Labour Party to retain the support of the business community, which it saw as crucial to achieving electoral success, has perhaps been the biggest obstacle to achieving true social partnership. As Heery (2005: 3) notes 'the inclusion of trade unionists on public bodies has been paltry when compared with the infusion of business representatives'.

A Comparative Evaluation

In addition to the debate surrounding the extent to which New Labour constitutes a break with the immediate past is the related question of what has happened to British industrial relations in comparative terms. There has been widespread interest in the varieties of capitalism literature (see Hall and Soskice, 2001) and whether New Labour's legislative programme has seen Britain consolidate itself as a liberal market economy or whether, through engaging with the social dimension of the EU, the UK is moving towards being a more coordinated market economy, characteristic of many states on the continent. The latter view can be supported by citing Britain's strengthening of both individual employment rights and collective participation channels to bring it more into line with the European norm. On the other hand, the reluctance to fully embrace EU directives and the retention of much of the Conservative neo-liberal legislation has led others to claim that the last eight years has done nothing to halt the 'Americanization' of the British labour market.

It is generally accepted that Tony Blair is an unenthusiastic European in terms of labour market reform (Dickens and Hall, 2003; Howell, 2004). That having been said, New Labour is undeniably less overtly Euro-sceptic than the Conservative governments that preceded it. One of the first actions of the new government in 1997 was to sign up to the Social Chapter, which exposed Britain to a stream of policy initiatives that had to be transposed into UK law. These included regulations on work–life balance, employment contracts, discrimination and worker participation. It is this last category which has excited most interest. With the implementation of European works councils and then a system of national works councils, via the Information and Consultation Directive, it has been argued that the British industrial relations system has moved to one of dual-channel representation, thus bringing it into line with the European norm.

The opposing view is that since the election of Labour in 1997, British labour market policy has not deviated from the neo-liberalism of the 1980s and 90s and that, as a consequence, Britain increasingly resembles the exemplar of deregulation, the United States (Howell, 2004). Evidence of this can be found in the minimal implementation of EU directives, which has been achieved through negotiating opt-outs and exclusions as in the case of working time, or by delaying their introduction, typified by the example of the Information and Consultation Directive, which will not be fully implemented until 2008. The government's credentials as enthusiastic members of the European project are further undermined when its refusal to sign up to further measures such as the Charter of Fundamental Rights is considered. Taken by itself Labour's reluctance to fully embrace the European model may not be enough to argue that it is neo-liberal in nature. However, when taken together with the fact that the majority of the Conservative legislative framework has remained intact, the argument that Britain is still closer to the American system of industrial relations than it is to the European norm becomes more persuasive.

Heery (2005) raises an interesting point when he argues that this debate may be informed by examining the union response to the New Labour programme since 1997. The 'Europeanization' thesis tends to be associated with a partnership oriented notion of unionism (Brown, 2000). The causal factors behind this move towards a more cooperative system of industrial relations lie in a recognition of the changing context within which IR operates. It can be argued that due to increasing product market competition, it is unsustainable for unions to represent their members' interests through adversarial bargaining alone. Furthermore, when the changing basis of competition is considered – the emergence of an alleged 'quality imperative' – then the potential for cooperative employment relations materializes. This combined with the changing legislative framework raises the possibility of 'productivity coalitions' between unions and employers, where unions may expand their influence into areas not traditionally covered by collective bargaining such as training and equal opportunities – all in the name of improving the viability of the business.

The alternative 'Americanization' hypothesis implies a correspondingly different trade union response. Heery and Adler (2004) claim that union movements faced with exclusionary state policies are likely to adopt policies that mobilize workers to protect their rights. They point out that whilst the legislative framework in the UK is not as hostile to unions as it is in the US, it falls far short of the notions of social partnership seen in Europe. Therefore, it is no coincidence that the UK stands out from the rest of Europe as being the only country in which the union movement have imported American organizing techniques. As Heery (2005: 5) comments 'the Americanization of public policy, on this reading, implies an Americanization of union response'.

Conclusions

This review has sought to evaluate the industrial relations programme of the first two terms of the Labour government in Britain. By looking at the spheres of individual employment regulation, collective employment law and partnership a pattern has emerged. That is to say a pattern of incoherence and inconsistency. In the area of individual employment law there have been significant changes such as the introduction of a statutory minimum wage, together with extensions of various protections for workers. However, these changes have not gone as far as many in the labour movement hoped, and have not altered Britain's position as the most lightly regulated labour market in Western Europe. This pattern of continuity and change is also apparent in the realm of collective employment regulation. Much has been made of the introduction of a statutory union recognition procedure. However, critics argue that the legislation is flawed and maintains significant barriers to unions gaining recognition. At the same time, the majority of the anti-union legislation of the 1980s and 90s has remained on the statute books, thus weakening the claim that New Labour represents a radical break in the system of industrial relations. As to where this leaves Britain in an international comparison, the picture is again mixed. There is evidence of a closer engagement with the social dimension of the European project, albeit with thinly disguised reluctance on the part of the British government, which at the same time has made no attempt to repeal the Conservative's US style neo-liberal legislation.

It is beyond the scope of this article to fully examine the causes for this apparent schizophrenia in New Labour's IR policy. Those who have attempted such an examination have either stressed the structural determinants of government action, essentially claiming that if you accept that Britain is characteristic of an economic system that is run by markets, then government policy is effectively path dependent (for a full exposition see Howell, 2004). The reverse is argued by writers like Hamann and Kelly (2003) who stress the autonomy of political action from economic or other constraints. They argue that political action is influenced by the desire to win elections and then the parliamentary rules which constrain the exercising of that power. It is argued that in order to achieve electoral success the Labour Party has had to shift emphasis away from the interests of trade unions and once in power, their two parliamentary landslides have served to further insulate them from calls from the union movement for radical legislative reform (Hamann and Kelly, 2003). Whatever the causes of New Labour's industrial relations programme, the conclusion that it lacks coherence and consistency remains. Indeed, it can be argued that what distinguishes New Labour's industrial relations programme from what went before it is this lack of consistency because by contrast the Conservative legislative programme of the 1980s and 90s now stands as a remarkably coherent labour market intervention.

References

Adnett, N. and Hardy, S. (2003) 'Reviewing the Working Time Directive: Rationale, Implementation and Case Law', *Industrial Relations Journal* 32(2): 114–25.

Arulampalam, W., Booth, A. and Bryan, M. (2004) 'Training and the New Minimum Wage', *Economic Journal* 114(March): C87–C94.

Brown, W. (2000) 'Putting Partnership into Practice in Britain', *British Journal of Industrial Relations* 38(2): 299–316.

Charlwood, A. (2004) 'The New Generation of Trade Union Leaders and Prospects for Union Revitalization', *British Journal of Industrial Relations* 42(2): 379–97.

Dickens, L. and Hall, M. (2003) 'Labour Law and Industrial Relations: A New Settlement?', in P. Edwards (ed.) *Industrial Relations: Theory and Practice*, pp.124–56. Oxford: Blackwell.

Hall, M. and Sisson, K. (1997) *Time for a Change? Coming to Terms with the EU Working Time Directive*. London and Coventry: IRS and IRRU.

Hall, P. and Soskice, D. (2001) *Varieties of Capitalism: The Institutional Foundations of Comparative Advantage*. Oxford: Oxford University Press.

Hamann, K. and Kelly, J. (2003) 'The Domestic Sources of Difference in Labour Market Policies,' *British Journal of Industrial Relations* 41(4): 639–63.

Heery, E. (2005) Trade Unionism under New Labour. Unpublished manuscript.

Heery, E. and Adler, L. (2004) 'Organizing the Unorganized', in C. M. Frege and J. Kelly (eds) *Varieties of Unionism: Strategies for Union Revitalization in a Globalizing Economy*, pp. 45–69. Oxford: Oxford University Press.

Hepple, B. (2000) 'Supporting Collective Bargaining: Some Comparative Reflections', in B. Towers and W. Brown (eds) *Employment Relations in Britain: 25 Years of the Advisory Conciliation and Arbitration Service*, pp. 153–61. Oxford: Blackwell.

Howell, C. (2004) 'Is There a Third Way for Industrial Relations?', *British Journal of Industrial Relations* 42(1): 1–22.

Hyman, R. (2003) 'The Historical Evolution of British Industrial Relations', in P. Edwards (ed.) *Industrial Relations: Theory and Practice*, pp. 37–57. Oxford: Blackwell.

Low Pay Commission (2003) *The National Minimum Wage. Fourth Report of the Low Pay Commission*. London: Stationery Office.

Machin, S. and Wilson, J. (2004) 'Minimum Wages in a Low-wage Labour Market: Care Homes in the UK', *Economic Journal* 114(March):C102–C109.

McIlroy, J. (2000) 'The New Politics of Pressure – The Trades Union Congress and New Labour in Government', *Industrial Relations Journal* 31(1): 2–16.

McKay, S. (2001) 'Between Flexibility and Regulation: Rights, Equality and Protection at Work', *British Journal of Industrial Relations* 39(2): 285–303.

Metcalf, D. (2004) 'The impact of the national minimum wage on the pay distribution, employment and training', *Economic Journal* 114(March): C84–C86.

Metcalf, D. (1999) 'The British National Minimum Wage', *British Journal of Industrial Relations* 37(2): 171–202.

Stewart, M. (2004) 'The Employment Effects of the National Minimum Wage', *Economic Journal* 114(March): C110–C116.

Terry, M. (2003) 'Employee Representation: Shop Stewards and the New Legal Framework', in P. Edwards (ed.) *Industrial Relations: Theory and Practice*, pp. 257–84. Oxford: Blackwell.

Waddington, J. (2003) 'Heightening Tension in Relations Between Trade Unions and the Labour Government in 2002', *British Journal of Industrial Relations* 41(2): 335–58.

Wood, S. (2000) 'From Voluntarism to Partnership: A Third Way Overview of the Public Policy Debate in British Industrial Relations', in H. Collins, P. Davies and R. Rideout (eds) *Legal Regulation of the Employment Relation*, pp. 111–53. Amsterdam: Kluwer Law International.

Wood, S. and Godard, J. (1999) 'The Statutory Union Recognition Procedure in the Employment Relations Bill: A Comparative Analysis', *British Journal of Industrial Relations* 37(2): 203–45.

9

Recent Industrial Relations Developments in China and Viet Nam: The Transformation of Industrial Relations in East Asian Transition Economies[1]

Chang-Hee Lee
ILO, Thailand

During the last decade, the industrial relations landscape in East Asia has experienced significant changes. The economic crisis in the late 1990s in Indonesia, Korea and Thailand (to a lesser extent, Malaysia and the Philippines), and the decade-long economic stagnation in Japan have altered the political economy of employment relations, bringing inevitable changes to labour markets and therefore industrial relations dynamism. However, most dramatic changes have taken place in the transition economies of East Asia, namely China, Viet Nam, Cambodia, Lao PDR and Mongolia. This article aims to review the transformation of industrial relations in the two most populous transition economies of East Asia, China and Viet Nam. These two countries were selected because of growing signs of divergent developments in industrial relations, despite similarities in their patterns of political and economic transition.

Industrial Relations Developments in 1990s: China and Viet Nam in the 1990s

China and Viet Nam share many common features in their approaches to economic and political reforms. Their economic reforms have taken gradualist approaches of restructuring state owned enterprises (SOEs) combined with a slow but steady opening-up of their markets in a clear contrast with the sweeping privatization seen in other former socialist economies of Central and Eastern European countries (CEEC). In the arena of political reform, both countries continue to maintain a monopoly of political power vested in the communist parties, which again distinguishes these countries from the former socialist economies of CEECs.

The patterns of industrial relations transformation in both countries mirror common characteristics in their transition. Workers do not have the right to freedom of association. The All China Federation of Trade Unions (ACFTU) in China and the Viet Nam General Confederation of Labour (VGCL) in Viet Nam continue to be the only officially sanctioned union organizations with close links to the communist parties. Known as transmission belts, these organizations have served as a part of state bureaucracies for decades before the economic transition, and assigned with the contradictory functions of representing the interests of both the workers and the Party-state. The economic reforms brought on market-based employment relations where the separation of interests between workers and employers became more obvious. It is in this new environment that the Parties and the unions have increasingly placed more emphasis on the role of unions to represent workers' legitimate rights and interests instead of just being a top-down transmission belt between the Party and workers.

Revisions of trade union laws (China in 1992 and Viet Nam in 1990), changes to the union constitutions (China and Viet Nam in 1993) and adoption of the new labour laws (China and Viet Nam in 1995) reflect the two countries' efforts to modernize industrial relations and redefine the role of trade unions in the new environment of market-based employment relations. The parallel development of legislative frameworks took place independently of each other. There is little evidence of mutual learning and influencing (Chan and Norlund, 1998). Rather, the timing of the reforms reflects similar challenges faced in the early days of market reforms in both countries.

Generally speaking, these legislative initiatives attempt to amalgamate new elements such as employment contracts, collective bargaining and agreements and new dispute settlement procedures with the socialist labour relations regime where there was supposed to be no line of separation between the interests of workers and employers, where unions acted as an intermediary between workers and managers, and where unions were expected to serve the Party's policies.

The introduction of modern elements of industrial relations such as collective bargaining and new dispute settlement machineries has created a space for the trade unions in both countries to start new experiments with collective bargaining at enterprise level and tripartite consultation at higher levels within the political limit of the socialist labour relations regime. In particular, another round of Trade Union Law revision in China (October 2001) and the Labour Code revision in Viet Nam (April 2002) has given further momentum for industrial relations actors to expand and accelerate the scope and pace of their experiments in both countries. And it is the recent industrial relations experiments which appear to lead to clearer signs of divergence. In the following sections, we will review the main developments of industrial relations experiments in both countries as well as their implications for future IR developments.

Tripartite Consultation Institutions and Processes in China and Viet Nam

Preemptive Corporatism Through Institutional Cloning of Tripartite Bodies in China

Industrial relations developments in China since 2000 can be described as a joint attempt at preemptive corporatism by the Party-state and the ACFTU. The revision of the Trade Union Law in 2001 neither altered the political environment for union operation nor addressed the representational deficiency of the trade unions at the workplace. However, it has opened up several new and significant institutional opportunities for the ACFTU to strengthen its influence vis-à-vis state administration at various levels by mandating tripartite consultation mechanisms. Articles 33 and 34 of the 2001 Trade Union Law provides a legal basis for unions' participation at the government policy level on a wide range of labour and social policy issues, and tripartite consultation at various levels on major issues of labour relations. Based upon these provisions, tripartite actors in China have begun to establish tripartite consultation committees (TCCs), starting from the creation of the National TCC in 2001.[2] The national TCC is headed by the vice-minister of the Ministry of Labour and Social Security (MOLSS), the vice-chairperson of the ACFTU and the vice-president of the CEC (China Enterprise Confederation). The TCC has been established to improve coordination among the three parties in their efforts to develop harmonious labour relations, reflecting the overriding concern of the Party-state to maintain social stability through better labour relations (Lee and Clarke, 2002).

As of December 2004, TCCs had been established in all provinces and most municipalities. Now tripartite joint efforts are being made to set up TCCs at district level. The pace at which TCCs have spread down to the lower levels of administration clearly indicates that this 'institutional cloning' of tripartite mechanisms was apparently conducted in a top-down manner. There is a certain degree of local variation in the actual operation of TCCs. For example, it has been reported that there are local TCCs (such as those in the Heilongjiang province) where broader labour policy issues such as employment and social security policy issues are discussed among the three parties. However, the author's field visits and discussions with tripartite actors in various localities suggest that TCC's mandate is generally limited to narrowly defined labour relations issues such as the promotion of collective bargaining, joint inspection of labour law enforcement and sometimes, new local regulations on industrial relations, as it is defined by the guidelines at the national level.

In spite of the apparent top-down bureaucratic manner, the institutionalization of TCCs has been a catalyst of recent industrial relations evolution in China. TCCs have become a major vehicle for spreading new practices of 'collective consultation on equal footing'[3] across localities and sectors. Figure 1 illustrates that the number of collective agreements has surged since 2001, which was the year that TCCs began to be established. According to ACFTU

Figure 1 *Enterprises with collective agreements*

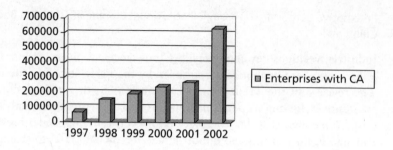

statistics, 103.5 million workers were said to be covered by collective agreements as of December 2003 (Zhang, 2005). The ACFTU has set a target of achieving 60 percent of collective bargaining coverage rate by the 2008 Beijing Olympic Games. Of course, sudden increases in collective agreements can be more easily explained by bureaucratic competition to meet targets, than by a real increase of collective bargaining. Most observers – both foreign and domestic, including some officials of the government and ACFTU – agree that there are serious deficiencies in the current collective bargaining system in terms of the quality of the agreements and of the bargaining process. Indeed, many collective agreements tend to be a little more than the replication of legal minimum working conditions with minor modifications, while the collective bargaining process tends to be a ritualistic preparation of joint documents with little or formalistic involvement of workers and without a genuine process of negotiation (Lee, Clarke and Li, 2004; Taylor, Chang and Li, 2003). However, as we will describe in the following sections, the concerted campaign for 'collective consultation' has created a new industrial relations dynamism in a significant number of enterprises in China, with a possibility of gradual transformation of workplace trade unions.

National Labour Politics in Viet Nam: The Emerging Articulation of Interests

Viet Nam has also recently established a tripartite consultation mechanism at national level in accordance with the 2002 Labour Code. The tripartite consultation body in Viet Nam differs from its Chinese counterpart in a number of significant ways.

Firstly, the national tripartite body in Viet Nam has a broader agenda for consultation, which covers virtually all issues related to labour policies including wages, social security, labour legislation and other industrial relations issues. This broader mandate of the national tripartite body generates more incentives for representatives of workers and employers to use this institutional channel for their influence over social and labour policy decision-making, while the National TCC in China, which has a narrower mandate, provides fewer incentives for representatives of workers and particularly employers to do so.

Institutional incentives for social actors to use the national tripartite body for their own interests are further enhanced by the fact that the tripartite body in Viet Nam has a higher political status than in China – the tripartite body is represented by heads of all tripartite actors (Labour Minister, the Chairwoman of VGCL and the President of Viet Nam Chamber of Commerce and Industries) – not just by the deputy heads as in China. Furthermore, the Prime Minister is obliged to have an annual conference with the heads of tripartite parties to discuss major social and labour policy issues of national significance.

Secondly, the tripartite interaction at a national level occasionally involves tense negotiations. An illustrative example is the tripartite debate on the overtime regulation. In 2002, VGCL succeeded in codifying their demand of limiting maximum overtime work to 200 hours per year into the revised Labour Code. At the last minute of the Labour Code revision process, however, VCCI and the textile and garment manufacturers' association (whose members faced the prospect of heightened competition due to the elimination of the export quota set by the Multi Fibre Agreement which expired by the end of 2004) fought back and gained an exemption clause for certain sectors allowing maximum 300 overtime hours per year subject to the Prime Minister's approval based upon consultation with VGCL and employers' representatives (article 69 of the 2002 Labour Code). Later, the textile and garment manufacturers achieved the exemption for their sector from the Prime Minister. This indicates that the tripartite processes in Viet Nam do not merely conform to and execute State-Party policies, but provide opportunities for articulating the interests of labour and management, which results in occasional tensions and compromises.

Employers in the Tripartite Process at National and Local Levels: China and Viet Nam

Though there are subtle differences between the ACFTU and VGCL regarding their perceived relations with the Party-state and workers, both unions have similar characteristics as the officially sanctioned monopoly union with very weak democratic links with their constituents at the workplace. Perhaps, the most illustrative dimension revealing the different organizational and representational foundations for tripartite interest articulation at national and local levels is associated with the status of collective employers in national labour politics and tripartite interaction in the two countries. To put it simply, the institutional cloning of TCCs has started to give a new meaning to the officially designated employers' organization in China, while the competition and cooperation between competing organizations of employers has given greater meaning to tripartism in Viet Nam.

In its attempt to replicate the tripartite structure down to municipal and district levels, China faces a significant obstacle – that is, the absence or underdevelopment of employers' organization at lower levels of administration. CEC (formerly known as China Enterprise Management Association) was established by the State Trade and Economic Commission (STEC) as China began to experiment with the decentralization of the management of SOEs at the beginning of the 1980s. Its purpose was to maintain links between STEC and the SOEs that had formerly been under the direction of the State Planning Commission. In 1998, STEC authorized CEC to act as the representative of all enterprises in industrial relations matters and in 1999 issued instructions to all provincial governments requiring them to delegate this authority to CEC (Lee and Clarke, 2002). The members of CEC at the national level were traditionally the largest SOEs that came under the jurisdiction of the national government. As reform progressed, branches of CEC were established in all provinces and numerous municipalities to cater for the smaller SOEs that came under the jurisdiction of provincial and municipal authorities.

This historical origin of CEC poses a problem for employers' representation – on both a horizontal and vertical scale. The horizontal dimension refers to the question of which business associations would represent entire employers in China, as CEC alone obviously lack representational capacity. There are a number of business associations in China, including CEC, *Gongshanglian* (the organization of local, private businesses) and various associations 'representing' foreign investors, joint ventures and other types of businesses. Among them, *Gongshanglian* is known to have the most powerful lobby capacity, due to its membership basis in local private sector, and equally importantly due to its seat in the National People's Congress and the National Political Consultative Body. Though CEC tries to become an umbrella organization of employers, for example, by appointing representatives of other business associations as deputy chairpersons of the CEC, there is little indication that these appointments improve inter-organizational coordination and cooperation. It appears that each organization enjoys its monopoly status within its territory, assigned by the relevant government authorities with little coordination among the associations. The vertical dimension of employers' representation in China is related to the fact that CEC does not have its branches at lower level of the administration where TCC has begun to be already set up. At the lower level of administration where CEC has no branches, the local branch of the STEC is appointed as an official representative agency of employers. In some districts, representatives of employers are 'elected' from influential employers of the localities as an interim measure until a CEC branch is established. In this regard, the state's imperative of replicating TCC has been driving the institutional 'implantation' of quasi 'employer' organizations' down to municipal and district levels in China.

On the other hand, the relationship between the evolution of tripartism and employers' organizations in Viet Nam is markedly different from China. Initially the government had planned to establish tripartite bodies not only at national level, but also at provincial level. But in the end the government had to set up a national consultation body due to competition and conflict between the VCA (Viet Nam Cooperative Alliance) which had its membership base in cooperative and small enterprises, and the VCCI (Viet Nam Chamber of Commerce and Industries) which represented relatively large size enterprises of various ownerships. The problem was that the VCCI had its branches only in a number of the most industrialized provinces, while its political and economic importance surpassed the VCA. On the other hand, the VCA had branches in all provinces but its influence had declined due to the collapse and dismantling of the cooperative sector. It was the VCCI which opposed the establishment of tripartite mechanisms at province level as it feared that it would lead to a situation where employers would be represented by the VCA in most provinces where the VCCI has no branches. The tripartite debate on the rules of selecting employers' representatives for tripartite consultation at provincial level is still underway.

A noteworthy fact is that, despite its limited geographical coverage, the VCCI has far stronger representational credentials than its Chinese counterpart, CEC: VCCI encompasses both SOEs and all types of non-public enterprises (local private, joint ventures and foreign ventures), and has close organizational links with foreign investors' associations as well as various sectoral business associations. The VCCI combines the function of the Chamber of Commerce and Industry with the function of employers' organization: the function of employers' organization is carried out by the Employers' Activities Bureau within the VCCI. This gives an organizational advantage to the VCCI in representing various interests of businesses and employers in tripartite consultation.

In addition to its competition with the VCA, there is both competition and cooperation between the VCCI and sectoral associations of businesses. This is more prominent in Southern Viet Nam where a number of semi-autonomous associations representing sectoral interests of local, private businesses are quite active (Nguyen and Stromseth, 2002). These sectoral associations sometimes compete with the VCCI for their political influence at local level. This is evident in the tripartite arbitration council in the Ho Chi Minh City (HCMC) where it is the HCMC association of industries which sit on the council, while it is usually either the VCCI or VCA which represents employers in the arbitration council of all other provinces. However, the competitive relations between the different associations also co-exist with cooperative relations. For example, the president of the textile and garment manufacturer association is also the chair of the VCCI's industrial relations committee. During the lobby for the exemption of the textile and garment sector regarding the overtime regulation, the VCCI worked closely with the textile and garment manufacturer's association.

This pattern of competition and cooperation between VCCI and other associations offers greater institutional opportunities for Viet Nam to channel and articulate the interests of employers through the official industrial relations process at supra enterprise level.

The Industrial Relations Process at Enterprise Level and its Interaction with Local Industrial Relations Actors in China and Viet Nam

Due to the legacy of trade unions' functions under socialist labour relations, trade unions at the enterprise level in both countries continue to be weak in their capacity to represent workers primarily through collective bargaining and industrial actions. Trade unions in China and Viet Nam continue to encompass all types of 'workers', including top managers. This originated from the nature of socialist employment relations where it was perceived that no conflicts of interests existed between the management and workers. This perception has easily become a convenient tool for management to dominate the workplace and control the unions in a new market environment. In both countries, the trade union leadership at the enterprise level is disproportionately dominated by staff members representing the management.

However, the recent industrial relations experiments and evolution at and above the enterprise level have begun to impact on the way enterprise unions function. In this section, we will review changes at the workplace level and the interaction between industrial relations actors at workplace and higher levels, and discuss its implications for the future development of industrial relations in the two countries.

Official Incorporation, Gradual Transformation of Workplace Unions and Containment of Un-official IR Actors in China

As we argued earlier, a series of legislation created space for new experiments of industrial relations within the political constraints of the Party-state in China and the establishment of TCC generated a new impetus for a nation-wide campaign for 'collective consultation on equal footing' at the enterprise level. Though the quality of collective agreements and the process of collective consultation remain problematic in the majority of workplaces in China, there is a sign that the new industrial relations dynamism may be occurring at a significant number of enterprises. Upon reviewing the outcome of their campaign for collective agreements in late 1990s, ACFTU cadres were frustrated with the fact that many collective agreements contained nothing more than the legal minimum. They realized that if this situation continued, collective consultation would not serve its original purpose of stabilizing labour relations at the workplace through improving working conditions for workers.

It was in this context that the ACFTU started a new campaign for wage negotiation, because it was too easy for trade union officials at the enterprise level, with the old socialist mindset, to regard collective agreements as another legal document to be signed off without actual consultation with their members and without genuine negotiations with their employers. It appears that the ACFTU's campaign for wage negotiation has created, to a limited extent, a new industrial relations dynamism. First, wage negotiation, by its nature, cannot result in the duplication of legal minimum conditions, as it is about negotiating new level of wages for workers. More importantly, wage negotiation creates a greater degree of immediate interest amongst workers in the conduct of wage negotiation in particular and the union's functions in general, because their vital interests are at stake. The author's field research confirms this pattern: wage negotiation increases interests and participation of union members in the union affairs, and in turn enterprise unions come under greater pressure to become more accountable to and more representative of their members.[4] It is reported by the ACFTU that 35.79 million workers were covered by wage agreements as of December 2003 (Zhang, 2005). Patterns of wage negotiations and their impacts on workplace industrial relations need to be further studied on a large scale.

However, it is safe to say that the ACFTU machinery as a union bureaucracy has been relatively effective in implementing the policies across the country, decided by the highest level of union hierarchy with a strong endorsement of the Party-state. Also, as seen in the case of the effects of wage negotiation, this concerted effort of preemptive incorporation may contribute to gradual strengthening of ACFTU unions at the workplace, by opening an opportunity for workers to participate in the official unions' orderly exercise of bargaining rights.

Whatever happens within the official system of industrial relations by the official industrial relations actors, however, a larger question remains unanswered: the rising tide of labour disputes. As Figure 2 shows, the incidence of labour disputes – both individual and collective – has been rapidly rising. The growth rate of labour disputes is almost three times higher than China's GDP growth rate. Figures 1 and 2 demonstrate that labour disputes have increased while collective agreements have spread at a similar or even higher rate. According to our respondents, there are very few collective disputes arising from either

Figure 2 *Number of labour disputes in China*

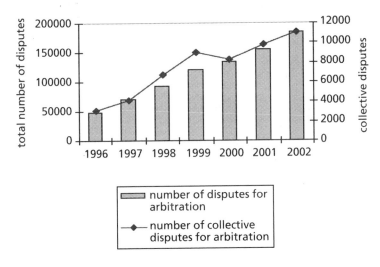

failure of negotiating new agreements (collective disputes over interests) or interpretation/application of the existing agreements (collective disputes over rights). There have been also few, if any, cases, brought to the local arbitration council by the official trade unions – they are almost always taken up by the aggrieved workers themselves, although they are occasionally supported by local legal aid centers (Zhou, 2004). However, the incidence of rank-and-file workers taking industrial action or protesting has been increasing. To the extent that the government admits the gravity of the situation, industrial action is often met with the harsh repression by public authorities. There is little evidence that the official trade unions intervene in defence of those workers' rights and interests.

This means that labour disputes have grown independently of the spread of collective bargaining, and that the official trade unions have so far failed to represent workers in the process of the disputes. This is a crucial failure for trade unions, which are supposed to represent workers at times of industrial conflict as well as channel conflicting interests through the collective bargaining process into a compromise solution. The clear demarcation between the official sphere of industrial relations and the unofficial actions of the aggrieved workers offers a proxy measure to assess the effectiveness of the preemptive corporatist attempt of the Party-state and the unions, combined with the strict sanctions imposed over workers' spontaneous actions outside the formal legal framework.

Autonomous Space for Spontaneous Solidarity at the Workplace and Tolerant Approach of the Party-state in Viet Nam

As we described earlier, there are few differences between the two countries in that both have ineffective enterprise trade unions with serious flaws in their representational capacity. Differences are found not in the functions of the enterprise trade unions, but in the 'organizational strength' of rank-and-file workers as well as in the approaches of the Party-state and the official trade unions at higher levels.

First, rank-and-file workers in Viet Nam have displayed a great degree of spontaneous solidarity, outside the official unions and the official legal framework, to defend and advance their rights and interests through organizing well coordinated strike actions. Since the adoption of the Labour Code in 1995, there have been more than 900 strikes, all of which were 'wildcat strikes' – i.e. strikes organized not by the official unions but by workers themselves, and without going through legal procedures. The author's field research found out that most of the wildcat strikes were not only well planned and coordinated, but were also participated in by a majority of the workers within the enterprises concerned. The so-called contagion effect of wildcat strikes illustrates the Vietnamese workers' ability to take well coordinated collective actions. For example, on December 28th 2005, 18,000 workers of a Taiwanese owned company in Linh Trung Processing Zone in Ho Chi Minh City went on a wildcat strike demanding a wage increase, which was immediately followed by simultaneous strikes in two other factories in the same Zone on the same issue on December 29th. This and other similar incidents indicate that Vietnamese workers have greater organizational capacity to mobilize and unite themselves through collective actions than their Chinese counterparts.

Second, what is also noticeably different from China is the response of the public authority to wildcat strikes. In Viet Nam the local labour administration will usually send its conciliators to investigate the situation and to resolve the strike situation by offering a compromise. The government's intervention tends to legitimatize workers' actions by arguing that workers' legitimate rights were infringed by employers and that therefore employers should accept legitimate demands of strikers. Of the 50 strikes in which we have information about the outcome, the workers' key demands were met in 48 cases (Lee, 2005). One foreign manager, who had been persuaded to meet the demands of his striking workers by a labour department official, complained to us that 'the government should be neutral but in fact they are a bit more on the workers' side'. Another foreign manager was quietly advised by a local government official not to take any retaliatory action such as dismissal against the strike leaders, as it would only provoke another round of strikes. Strong public support for workers' collective actions, helped by local media's favourable coverage of the collective actions, also generates pressures on the local government to intervene in favour of workers.

Third, trade unions at higher organizational level in Viet Nam tend to display stronger support for workers on strikes than their counterparts in China. Local trade union cadres, who usually accompany the government conciliators, often sympathize with workers' causes and put pressure on the management side to accept reasonable demands of strikers, while also persuading workers to return to work. In response to the above strikes in Linh Trung Processing Zone in December 2005, VGCL at provincial and national levels came out openly on the strikers' side, criticized the government's failure in raising the minimum wage, and demanded the government to raise the minimum wage.

The strong solidarity of workers, the tolerant attitude of the public authorities and the supportive response of the general public to workers' collective actions, as well as the sympathetic and semi-autonomous behaviour of higher-level trade union organizations all serve to differentiate Viet Nam from China.

Spontaneous Solidarity, Workers' community and Elites' Perception of People's Power

As Chan and Wang (2004) noted, a greater degree of solidarity and organizational capacity of Vietnamese workers to take collective action compared to their Chinese counterparts can be ascribed to a number of factors. First, the household registration system (*hukou*) in China renders Chinese migrant workers in urban factories very vulnerable to factory management, because migrant workers can neither leave the company nor apply for another job if the management decides to take away certain essential documents from the workers. In Viet Nam, though this system exists, it has never been enforced to the extent that workers become vulnerable to management abuses. Second, a majority of Chinese migrant workers live in company dormitories, which seriously restricts their freedom and reduces the possibility of workers socializing and exchanging information with workers in other factories. In Viet Nam, most workers, including rural migrant workers, commute from local community residential areas where they form a common identity and share information on working conditions of different factories in the locality. During the author's field research, a number of foreign factory managers and local government officials stated that workers in the local community frequently exchange information on working conditions of different factories in the industrial zone. This creates a situation of information asymmetry between the workers and their foreign managers – where workers possess more information than management about conditions in other workplaces – this partly explains why there have been the 'contagion' phenomena of wildcat strikes in a number of factories in the economic zones.

In addition to the above factors, government officials whom we interviewed expressed the view that politicians and government officials should take great care in dealing with workers, because workers are powerful enough to resist government policies in what is still perceived as a workers' state. The ruling elite's perception on and respect for the people's power seems to have originated from the experience of a half-century of war as well as a traditionally strong sense of autonomous community.

Another key factor differentiating Vietnamese workers from Chinese would be the fact that Viet Nam's Labour Code guarantees the right to strike. Though the right to strike is circumscribed by cumbersome procedures in Viet Nam, the legal recognition of the right to strike helps to legitimatize the workers' collective actions, and eliminate the political sensitivity and fears which dominate any public discussion on the subject in China.[5]

Tentative Conclusions and Future Prospects

As noted earlier, the trade unions at the enterprise level in both countries share similar weaknesses and flaws in terms of their capacity to represent workers through collective bargaining and industrial actions. Yet there are signs of divergence between the two countries.

China has adopted preemptive corporatist strategies in a top-down manner. This is evident in the institutional cloning of tripartite structures at all levels and systematic promotion of collective consultation and wage negotiation through the hierarchies of the Party-state and union machineries. As in the case of the effects of wage negotiation on the gradual strengthening of workplace unions' representational and bargaining capacity, this preemptive corporatist strategy seems to have yielded some positive results. But there seem to be clear limits to the preemptive corporatist strategies: first, in order for tripartite mechanisms to work as an institutional process through which labour relations is coordinated and conflicting interests are articulated, there should be collective social actors who are capable of articulating their constituents' interests and views. However, this condition is lacking in China on both union and employer sides. Compared with Viet Nam, China does not have cohesive employers' organizations which can actively articulate views and interests of different employers, and channel them through the official industrial relations process. The absence or weakness of cohesive employers' organizations will reduce the institutional dynamism of tripartite interaction.

Another limitation of the Chinese approach to labour relations is reflected in the rapidly growing number of labour disputes. The corporatist strategy has not so far yielded a meaningful improvement in conflict management. The aggrieved workers' direct actions in the form of either strikes or demonstrations continue to be either suppressed or even repressed. As an integral part of the Party-state apparatus, the ACFTU continues to closely align itself with the interests of Party-state apparatus. While this gives the advantage of having some leverage over the Party's decisions regarding the unions' desire of expanding their sphere of influence, for example, through the newly established system of tripartite consultation, it may also define the limit on how far they can reach out to workers and play their representative role as a collective voice of workers.

By contrast with China, Viet Nam displays elements of the intrinsic organizational dynamism of tripartite interaction. Competition and cooperation between and within tripartite parties characterizes the nature of tripartite interaction in Viet Nam – particularly on the side of collective employers. National labour politics are being shaped by social actors who pursue their own goals which reflect views and interests of their constituents. At supra enterprise level, Vietnamese trade unions display more active support for and sympathy with workers' causes than their counterparts in China. Chan and Wang (2004) suggest it may be due to more autonomy VGCL enjoys vis-à-vis state apparatus and therefore more alignment of VGCL with workers than AFCTU does.

Despite political and social factors generating forces for divergence between two countries, representational deficiencies continue to characterize industrial relations and trade unionism at the workplace level in both China and Viet Nam. It is yet to be seen if political and social factors will create different opportunity structures for industrial relations actors to develop distinctive industrial relations at the enterprise level. In this respect, it is important to note that the governments in China and Viet Nam have a plan to improve the regulatory framework for industrial relations in coming years – the revision of industrial relations chapters of the 2002 Labour Code in Viet Nam and the reform of dispute settlement machineries in China. A critical question would be how these regulatory changes will redefine industrial relations process at the workplace and the interaction of industrial relations actors at the enterprise level and beyond.

Notes

1 This article is based upon the author's field researches, carried out in China (May 2002 and October 2004) and Viet Nam (April 2001 and November 2004). In each trip, the author had a series of in-depth interviews with industrial relations actors at enterprise, municipality, province and national level. The first field research in Beijing, Dalian and Chengdu in China (May 2002) was undertaken jointly with Simon Clarke and Anita Chan, and the second field research in Hanoi and Ho Chi Minh City, Viet Nam (November 2004) was carried out together with Simon Clarke and Do Quynh Chi. The views expressed in this article does not necessarily reflect the views of the International Labour Office where the author is working as an industrial relations specialist.

2 It is to be noted, however, that tripartite consultation mechanism was established in a number of municipalities (such as Nanjing and Dalian) on experimental basis in the late 1990s before the establishment of the National TCC.

3 In China, the term 'collective consultation on equal footing' is used in its labour legislation instead of collective bargaining, though the term 'collective bargaining' has recently begun to be used more frequently among industrial relations actors in China.

4 In one small local private company which the author visited, the enterprise union, upon receiving instruction from municipal federation of trade unions, conducted wage negotiation initially with little involvement of his members. Upon learning the outcomes of wage negotiation, many of the union members expressed their discontent with the unions. In the second year of the wage negotiation, workers began to visit the union chair's office with their demands and grievances. In the meantime, the union chair decided to get a 'workers' representative' into his union committee so as to make his union more representative vis-à-vis its members. In the 2004 wage negotiation, the union chairman carried out systematic consultation of his members before wage negotiation with the employer. This case suggests that the national campaign for wage negotiation has positive effect on union governance at the workplace level.

5 In this respect, different terminologies regarding collective bargaining – 'collective consultation on equal footing' in China and collective bargaining in Viet Nam – are not just a question of linguistic differences. This difference is associated with both countries' different legislative regulation on strikes – it is legally recognized in Viet Nam while not in China.

References

Chan, A. and Norlund, I. (1998) 'Vietnamese and Chinese Labour Regimes: On the Road to Divergence', *The China Journal* 40(July): 173–97.

Chan, A. and Wang, H. (2004) 'The Impact of the State on Workers' Conditions – Comparing Taiwanese Factories in China and Viet Nam', *Pacific Affairs* 77(4): 629–46.

Lee, C.-H. (2005) ILO Discussion Paper: Strikes and Industrial Relations in Viet Nam, Bangkok, unpublished manuscript.

Lee, C.-H. and Clarke, C. (2002) 'Towards a System of Tripartite Consultation in China', *Asia Pacific Business Review* 9(2): 61–80.

Lee, C.-H., Clarke, S. and Li, Q. (2004) 'Collective Consultation and Industrial Relations in China', *British Journal of Industrial Relations* 42(2): 235–54.

Nguyen, P. Q. T. and Stromseth, J. R. (2002) *Business Associations in Viet Nam: Status, Roles and Performance*. Hanoi: The Asia Foundation.

Taylor, B., Chang, K. and Li, Q. (2003) *Industrial Relations in China*. Northampton, Massachusetts: Edward Elgar Publishing Limited.

Zhang, J.-G. (2005) Institutional achievements and future prospect of collective bargaining in China, unpublished paper.

Zhou, X.-L. (2004) 'Woguo Laodong Zhengyi Xietiao Jizhide Shijian Yu Sikao' (Practices and Thought on Labour Dispute Coordination Mechnanisms in China), in B. F. Guan (ed.) *Zhongguo Laodong Zhengyi Xianzhuang Wenti Yu Sikao (Labour Disputes in China: Current situation, problems and thoughts)*, pp. 190–202. Beijing: Zhongguo Congren Chubanshe.

Index

THE INDUSTRIAL RELATIONS SOCIETY IN AUSTRALIA

The Industrial Relations Societies bring together representatives of management, the trade unions, the government services and the professions, together with specialists in the various academic disciplines concerned with industrial relations, and seek in their activities to develop an integrated approach to industrial relations. Each member's subscription includes payment for the *Journal of Industrial Relations*. Further particulars may be obtained from the honorary secretaries in each state.

INDUSTRIAL RELATIONS SOCIETY OF AUSTRALIA

The Industrial Relations Society Of Australia is a federation of the Industrial Relations Societies of the Australian Capital Territory, New South Wales, Victoria, Queensland, South Australia, Western Australia, Tasmania, the Northern Territory and Papua New Guinea. *President:* Susan Barrera *Vice Presidents:* Alex Allars, Colleen Atkinson, Russell Lansbury *Immediate Past President:* Cheryl-Anne Laird *Hon Secretary/Treasurer:* Joe Cantanzariti, GPO Box 1557, Sydney 2001 *Assistant Treasurer:* Jon Hanlon

INDUSTRIAL RELATIONS SOCIETY OF THE AUSTRALIAN CAPITAL TERRITORY

President: Sean McDonnell *Vice President:* Alex Allars *Immediate Past President:* Bob Cook *Treasurer:* James Morris *Secretary:* Michael Beardsley, PO Box 196, Civic Square, Canberra ACT 2608 *Patron:* Comm Barbara Deegan (AIRC Canberra)

INDUSTRIAL RELATIONS SOCIETY OF NEW SOUTH WALES

President: WR (Dick) Grozier *Vice Presidents:* Joe Cantanzariti, Russell Lansbury, Alastair Macdonald *Immediate Past President:* Greg Harrison *Secretary:* Christine Badcock, PO Box 74, Oatlands NSW 2117 *Treasurer:* Jon Hanlon *Patron:* The Hon Justice PR Munro
Newcastle Branch: *Chairperson:* Catherine Wilkinson *Honorary Secretary:* Allan Foster, PO Box 393, Newcastle 2300 *Assistant Secretary/Treasurer:* Greg Kerr

INDUSTRIAL RELATIONS SOCIETY OF VICTORIA

President: Frank Parry SC *Vice Presidents:* Geoff Fary, Kris Waite, Brian Lacy SDP, Elsa Underhill *Immediate Past President:* Julie Hansen *Secretary:* Natascha Boehm, c/- Australian Industry Group, 20 Queens Road, Melbourne VIC 3004 *Assistant Secretary:* Sally Hewitson *Treasurer:* Leigh Stewart *Assistant Treasurer:* Brendan Johnson *Patron:* Justice Geoffrey Giudice, President AIRC

INDUSTRIAL RELATIONS SOCIETY OF QUEENSLAND

President: Cheryl-Anne Laird *Vice Presidents:* Pat Knight, John Merrell, Tom Schulz *Immediate Past President:* Peter Garske *Secretary:* Dale Himstedt, GPO Box 361, Brisbane QLD 4001 *Treasurer:* Cathy Bray *Administrator:* Megan Fahy *Patron:* Comm Ken Bacon

INDUSTRIAL RELATIONS SOCIETY OF SOUTH AUSTRALIA

President: Peter Hampton *Vice President:* Craig Stevens *Immediate Past President:* Chris White *Secretary:* Rodger Prince, PO Box 62, Mitcham Shopping Centre, SA 5062 *Treasurer:* David Johns *Secretariat:* Ian Fiddian

INDUSTRIAL RELATIONS SOCIETY OF WESTERN AUSTRALIA

President: Kim Richardson *Vice Presidents:* Natalie Van Der Waarden, Melanie Binet *Immediate Past President:* Susan Barrera *Secretary:* Kelly O'Rourke, PO Box 6276, East Perth WA 6893 *Treasurer:* Marija Muccilli

INDUSTRIAL RELATIONS SOCIETY OF TASMANIA

President: DP Patricia Leary *Vice President:* Robert Flanagan *Immediate Past President:* Lily Burgess *Secretary:* Greg Cooper, c/-39–41 Davey Street, Hobart TAS 7000 *Treasurer:* Mark Watson

INDUSTRIAL RELATIONS SOCIETY OF THE NORTHERN TERRITORY

President: Colleen Atkinson *Vice President:* Samantha Miles *Immediate Past President:* Renate Mohrbach *Secretary / Public Officer:* Linda Blair, PO Box 1292, Darwin NT 0801 *Treasurer:* Anna McGill *Assistant Secretary / Treasurer:* Chris Hancock *Patron:* Comm Brendan Eames

EDITORS OF THE JOURNAL OF INDUSTRIAL RELATIONS

1959–1974	Kingsley Laffer (University of Sydney)
1974–1991	John Niland (University of New South Wales)
1991–1999	Braham Dabscheck (University of New South Wales)
1999–2005	Ron Callus and Russell Lansbury (University of Sydney)
2005–2010	Bradon Ellem and Russell Lansbury (University of Sydney)

PRESIDENTS OF THE INDUSTRIAL RELATIONS SOCIETY OF AUSTRALIA

The following individuals have served as President of the Industrial Relations Society of Australia since its inception in 1964. Details show the professional position held at the time of election together with state or territory of the relevant constituent society.

2006	Susan Barrera, Chief of Staff, Department of Premier and Cabinet, Western Australia
2005	Cheryl-Anne Laird, Associate Director, Livingstones, Queensland
2004	Michael Butler, Principal, HR + WorkLaw, Victoria
2003	Stephen Dowd, Partner, Piper-Alderman, South Australia
2002	Neil McHattie, Deputy Industrial Registrar, Australian Industrial Registry, Northern Territory
2001	Christine Short, Consultant, Western Australia
2000	Ed Davis, Professor, Macquarie University, New South Wales
1998/99	Hugh Armstrong, Conciliation Officer, WorkCover Service, Victoria
1997/98	Christine Hayward, Deputy Industrial Registrar, Australian Capital Territory
1996/97	Trevor Small, Manager Employment Services, Brambles Australasia, Queensland
1995/96	Sharon Woon, Senior Industrial Officer, Commonwealth Department of Industrial Relations, Northern Territory
1994/95	William Holdsworth, Consultant, South Australia
1993/94	Peter Halton, Secretary, Finance Sector Union, Tasmania
1992/93	Jack Gregor, Commissioner, Western Australian Industrial Relations Commission
1991/92	Tim Moore, Minister, New South Wales Parliament, New South Wales
1990/91	Colin G. Polites, Deputy President, Australian Industrial Relations Commission, Victoria
1989/90	Tom Barton, Secretary, Trades and Labour Council of Queensland
1988/89	Roy Hegarty, Deputy Industrial Registrar, South Australia
1987/88	Brian Brooks, Associate Professor, University of New South Wales
1986/87	Jim Coleman, Commissioner, Australian Conciliation and Arbitration Commission, Western Australia
1985/86	Gerry Lane, Deputy Director, Australian Chamber of Manufacturers, Victoria
1984/85	Noel Shepherd, Secretary, Merchant Service Guild of Australia, Queensland
1983/84	James Brassil, Chairman, National Occupational Health and Safety Commission, Australian Capital Territory
1982/83	John Niland, Professor, University of New South Wales
1981/82	Keith Marshall, President, Industrial Relations Commission of Victoria
1980/81	John Cross, Employee Relations Manager, Mitsubishi, South Australia
1979/80	David McLeish, Secretary, Electrical Trades Union of New South Wales
1978/79	Lionel Ledlie, Employee Relations Manager, Castlemaine Perkins, Queensland
1977/78	Edward Sykes, Professor, University of Melbourne, Victoria
1976/77	Owen Pamplin, Chairman, Tasmanian Wages Board
1975/76	Vic Techritz, Controller of Employer Relations, Mobil Oil, Victoria
1974/75	Harry Krantz, Secretary, Federated Clerks Union, South Australia
1972/74	John Moore, President, Australian Conciliation and Arbitration Commission
1971/72	Keith Hancock, Professor of Economics, Flinders University, South Australia
1969/71	Lindsay Bowes, Secretary, Department of Labour and Industry, South Australia
1967/69	George Polites, Director General, Confederation of Australian Industry, Victoria
1966/67	Norm Thom, President, Labour Council of New South Wales
1965/66	John Kerr, Barrister, New South Wales
1964	Norm Thom, President, Labour Council of New South Wales